# FACES
OF
# GENEROSITY

# TABLE OF CONTENT

# CORPORATE PROFILE

Founded in 1979, Ronald Blue & Co. is one of the largest independent fee-only wealth management firms in the United States with a network of 13 branch offices, serving clients through four distinct divisions. The firm provides comprehensive financial strategies based on biblical wisdom designed to enrich the lives of clients across the wealth spectrum in these key areas:

- Financial, retirement, estate, and trust planning
- Investment management and solutions
- Family office services
- Philanthropic counsel and strategies
- Business consulting
- Institutional client services

## BRANCH OFFICE LOCATIONS

| | |
|---|---|
| Atlanta, GA | Montgomery, AL |
| Baltimore, MD | Nashville, TN |
| Charlotte, NC | Orange County, CA |
| Chicago, IL | Orlando, FL |
| Holland, MI | Phoenix, AZ |
| Houston, TX | Seattle, WA |
| Indianapolis, IN | |

## CONTACT INFORMATION

Web:　www.ronblue.com

Mail:　300 Colonial Center Parkway
　　　　Suite 300
　　　　Roswell, GA 30076

Phone:　1-800-841-0362

Fax:　770-280-6001

# INTRODUCTION

I'm excited that this *Faces of Generosity* book is in your hands! Over the 35 years I have been in this business, the privilege of working with clients like those featured in this book has been one of the greatest gifts. I owe a special debt of gratitude to them for the time and effort they spent with our team making this book a reality. These contributors are a small sampling of thousands like them who are having an impact on this world through their generosity. I'm continually inspired not only by the stories in this book, but by all of our clients who are willing to share their time, talents, and treasure in ways that help others.

One of my passions in life is promoting giving and stewardship, but I haven't always been a generous giver. I grew up in a family where the only giving I saw was a few dollars placed in the church offering plate. Later in life, I learned how transitory life can be and how foolish it was to think I could actually "keep" possessions. Once I started to "let go" and realize that it all belongs to God anyway, I developed a more generous spirit and mindset. Giving has become a joyful, integral part of my life.

This transition took time and intentionality. First, I started by keeping a couple of $50 bills in my wallet. Whenever I saw someone having a bad day — the young lady at the dry cleaners, the UPS man, a waitress, or the landscaper whose mower had broken — I could respond to needs as God brought them across my path. Second, I challenged myself to give more to the church. Would giving 10% extra be that hard on my financial situation, and would I even miss it? Third, I budgeted a certain amount of funds to go to unexpected charitable giving opportunities or ministry needs as they came up. Let God show you what letting go and being generous will look like for you. If you are going to err on one side or the other, err on the side of generosity. You won't regret it!

Ronald Blue & Co.'s bedrock verse is **1 Timothy 6:17-19,** *"Instruct those who are rich in this present world not to be conceited or to fix their hope on the uncertainty of riches, but on God, who richly supplies us with all things to enjoy. Instruct them to do good, to be rich in good works, to be generous and ready to share, storing up for themselves the treasure of a good foundation for the future, so that they may take hold of that which is life indeed."* When we unpack this verse, we learn that:

- Though we may not consider ourselves "rich," if we have more than we need, the Bible says that we are indeed rich.
- To give is to convey to another; to transfer; to not keep.
- To keep means to retain in our possession; to maintain; to try not to lose or part with; to protect, guard and preserve; to secure against loss, to keep in the same state, to save from destruction and to make secure.

The rich farmer in Luke 12 was called a *fool* because he was not generous or rich toward God. In the book, *He Is No Fool,* Jim Elliott says, *"He is no fool who gives what he cannot keep to gain what he cannot lose."* A wise person sends it on ahead by being generous instead of trying to keep it here on this earth.

In Matthew 6, we find that if we try to keep our resources, "moth and rust will destroy and thieves will break in and steal." Because heaven is the only place where our resources are secure, Paul gave his instructions to store up a good foundation for the future.

Remember that giving benefits both the recipient and the giver. In our firm, we have found that generosity and financial freedom are inextricably linked. We've observed that the folks who enjoy the most freedom and joy in life are those who pursue a generous lifestyle. It's a way of living that allows you to hold everything you own — including your time and talents — with an open hand.

I hope that as you read this book you too will begin to experience the joy that giving can bring to your life. Take heart in how valuable your life is and the positive impact you can have on others. The more you can give away and adopt a mindset of sharing, the more true meaning you'll find. Thanks for being a face of generosity in a world that needs it.

Russ Crosson
President/CEO, Ronald Blue & Co.

# ONE

A SIMPLE
# STICK OF
CHEWING
# GUM

**KARAN & DAVID GETTLE**
*Indianapolis, Indiana*

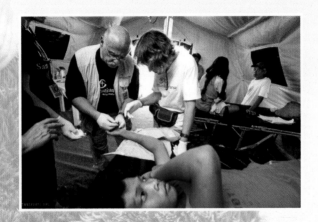

David Gettle, M.D. went into medicine because, like many health professionals, he simply wanted to help people. He specialized in emergency medicine because he wanted to help others who were in critical, life-threatening circumstances. What he didn't realize was how profoundly he would be changed by some of his experiences.

During David's medical school training, he had the opportunity to work in a free clinic in inner-city Indianapolis. One day, after treating and releasing a young patient at the clinic, the child's father came to him and gave him what he had to give . . . a stick of chewing gum. "I was just so humbled — here we are giving medical care to people who can't afford to pay and could otherwise not receive care and this man offered me a stick of his gum. It was a huge act of generosity. I think about it to this day. He will never know how many people were impacted by his act of generosity to me." A true, pay-it-forward moment began. And then disaster struck — literally.

> What he didn't realize was how profoundly he would be changed by some of his experiences.

David had always been attracted to the work of World Medical Mission, the medical arm of Samaritan's Purse, which offered three-week volunteer trips throughout the world. But the organization wasn't seeking emergency and trauma physicians, David's specialty, until 1999, when he saw in their newsletter a specific request for professionals in emergency medicine. "I picked up the phone and called them. About six weeks later, I got off a plane in Macedonia and headed to the city of Gjakova, Kosovo, which had come under heavy bombing by NATO forces. True atrocities against humans were going on — the results were thousands of refugees and internally displaced people who had nothing. We went to what was left of the old town — it was still smoldering from an attack. Needless to say, I had never worked in a war zone. But now I had to get an emergency room up and running in one, despite the fact there was only very sporadic electricity and precious few supplies. We even had to use batteries to run monitors and other medical equipment. I saw injuries I'd never seen before, such as those from landmines. It was truly an eye-opening experience."

After his return to the U.S., David made plans for a visit to Ethiopia on a six-month sabbatical from his position as vice president of medical affairs. That was when God began whispering to him that it might be time for a change from his current position. Very shortly after, he was working full-time for Samaritan's Purse, a Christian international relief organization. "That was what God told me I needed to be doing — and I knew He was right," says David.

David's most challenging experiences were in Haiti and South Sudan. The relief teams were urgently called to Haiti due to a devastating earthquake and were met with enormous human casualties and a seriously damaged infrastructure. In South Sudan during their civil war, David recalls, "We could see the flash and hear the booms. They flew us out the next day. Those are the kinds of situations where we had to cover the people in prayer, because there was little more we could offer them than to show the love of God. In Kosovo, I learned you have to hit your knees before you hit the wall, because you cannot do this by yourself. I found out how truly dependent on God you have to be."

> "I found out how truly dependent on God you have to be."

In Bam, Iran, a stuffed teddy bear made the difference that medical care couldn't after a 6.6 magnitude earthquake in December 2003, which killed more than 30,000 people. "So many people had nothing," says David. "We were, of course, a Christian aid group working among a group of Muslims. One father took me to his daughter, who had a very serious spinal injury. There was little we could do other than get her name and location and turn the information into a central coordinating center, but we did give her a teddy bear. The girl's mother and other women began crying, but not because we couldn't help her. Her father told us, 'It is because you gave her a teddy bear.' We were able to show compassion, which meant a lot to them."

During the past 10 years, David has, in his words, "been truly blessed to go to the largest international disasters," both natural and man-made ones: the tsunami in Banda Aceh, Indonesia, the refugee crisis in civil war-torn South Sudan, the war in Iraq, an earthquake in Haiti, and most recently the earthquake in Ecuador. "When we go in, we start working immediately. We don't go in to do an assessment, come back, and say 'Here's what needs to be done.' We're doing it — right then."

Karan Gettle experienced God's hand in a different way than her husband. Not allowed to accompany him on his numerous international medical trips because of the level of danger, and with absences of four to eight weeks, she stayed home — worried, of course, but "I always had peace beyond understanding. I never questioned that he was going where he was supposed to be. We never had a moment of hesitation that he should go. And, I've always had plenty of prayer warriors who have been here for me. They pray for his safety, for the activities of the team, and for the people he's serving. It's a 'front line' of a different kind. We're thrilled with how these decades of David's work in crisis areas have changed us both. It has made us so dependent on the Lord."

The Gettles note that you don't have to fly halfway around the world to help others in need. The couple works with an inner-city organization in Indianapolis, gathering in a parking lot on Sunday afternoons distributing food and clothing to families, playing with kids or taking them trick-or-treating. "Whatever you can do to help people in crisis or transition — well, all I can say is you'll receive blessings that you wouldn't have imagined. I'm reminded of that every time I think of that stick of chewing gum from many years ago," says David.

# TWO

# RUNNING ON
# EMPTY
## UNTIL A
# JOURNEY
## WITH THE
# MESSIAH

---

**MICHAEL BELK**
*Atlanta, Georgia*

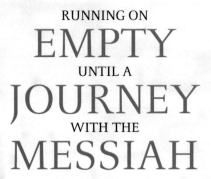

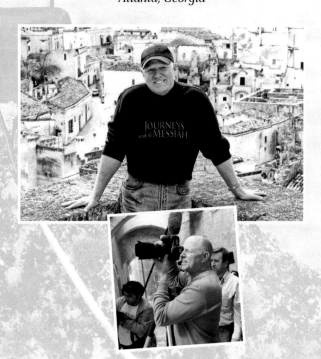

By the age of 42, Michael Belk was a renowned fashion photographer who traveled the globe internationally working with some of the biggest names in the fashion business. His work appeared in top publications such as Vogue, Elle, GQ, and Vanity Fair. He had achieved success that he could have only dreamed of when he first picked up a camera at the age of 20. By the age of 42, Michael Belk was also an empty vessel.

"My life was defined by great excitement and huge success, but very little substance," says Michael. "I was running on empty. Something was missing."

It certainly wasn't career accomplishments that were missing.

> "My life was defined by great excitement and huge success, but very little substance."

Michael grew up in central Florida, working in retail clothing in high school and college. Although he planned a career in the fashion industry and worked as a sales executive for Gant, a popular men's clothing line in the 1960s and 1970s, photography snagged his soul. Combining his gift for photography with a natural sense for sales and a little marketing savvy, Michael created catalogs and print collateral and, eventually, advertising campaigns throughout the clothing industry. His clients included such high-profile names as J. Crew, Nautica, Talbots, and Christian Dior. With his unique style, quality of products, speed of delivery and value, his business and his reputation grew. He was the man behind the camera, the creative director, and the account executive for his own boutique fashion advertising agency, Michael Belk & Company. "I was doing something I loved while traveling the world, working with many great models and crews in the industry," says Michael. "But it wasn't enough." It also had taken a toll on his personal life — fueled by his ego and his lifestyle.

In a very dark place, Michael had a visitor one day. "I felt the absolute presence of God in my room. He asked me: 'More of your way? Or would you like to try mine?' I decided I wanted to try God's way."

Expecting immediate restoration of a weary soul would have been too much to expect, but a change was underway. "The real journey to know my Lord and

Savior had begun," says Michael. So in 1993, Michael took a break to begin work on an idea for a book he believed could be used in point-of-sale retail marketing. He sold the concept to Champion Sportswear, an Olympic sponsor for the 1994 Winter Olympics. The book, *Beyond the Sport, The Victory Within,* included photographs and told inspirational stories of Peggy Fleming, Scott Hamilton, Eric Heiden, and other American Winter Olympians, selling 25,000 copies. 1993 was also the year that he was re-united with, and married, his college sweetheart, Cheryl.

> "I set out to create the images
> that would depict Jesus'
> timeless messages
> from a fresh perspective."

Returning to Florida in 2004, Michael opened a fine art photography gallery in a resort community. Sensing that God had greater plans beyond his fashion career, he began pursuing an idea that he believes God put on his heart. In 2008, Michael closed the gallery, put his fashion photography career on hold, and took a bold leap of faith.

"Sometimes the only information we have about Christianity is distorted," says Michael. "We may know Christianity from our childhood or from television. I wanted people to put aside ideas they had about Jesus and simply listen to what He had to say. It was an all-in response to one of God's questions: 'What are you doing with all that I gave you? Are you using it all for yourself or sharing it with others?'"

The dream that God placed on Michael's heart was a series of fine art photos that would depict many of the messages Jesus came to share with us 2,000 years ago and the relevance of those messages today. "The project was an enormous undertaking. We headed to Italy to the ancient city of Matera and found an amazing Italian actor to play Jesus. The project included a cast of more than 100 extras — and a budget that tripled by project's end. But this was such important work. I set out to create the images that would depict Jesus' timeless messages from a fresh perspective. My desire was to ignite a new passion in people, one with a depth of feeling and emotion. Some of the images are enlightening and full of hope, others are very challenging."

*Journeys with the Messiah* combines Jesus' parable-style teaching with the old adage, "A picture is worth a thousand words," resulting in a beautiful and engaging collection of photographic artwork that is helping people "see" the relevance of Jesus in their lives today. It presents Him from a fresh, innovative, and inviting perspective.

"From the beginning, we sensed we were on a mission to help people relate to Jesus in simple, relevant, and non-religious terms," says Michael. "So we created photographs that depict a 1st Century Jesus, in a 1st Century setting, and then we added a 21st Century element. Our desire is that these images will create a passion in the lives of believers and non-believers to know Him or know Him more. We've received testimonies from around the world that give evidence that *Journeys'* images provide a bold, yet comfortable, way for Christians to open conversations with others about Jesus. Just hang a picture in your home or office of Jesus walking down a country road with a Nazi, and I guarantee that you will not be the one who starts the conversation. But you will have an opportunity to talk with someone about Jesus' message of forgiveness."

The 45 images in *Journeys With the Messiah,* first published in 2009, have been interpreted beyond the limited-edition, signed, and numbered fine art originals to include a coffee table book, behind-the-scenes DVD, note cards, and posters. *Journeys* has received accolades from around the world, including from Dr. Charles Stanley of In Touch Ministries in Atlanta. Michael travels to churches and other venues to present the images in an exciting audio/visual presentation. He has also developed a sermon package and study curriculum and plans a mobile app and a pocket-size book. For Michael, the bottom line is not that he is in the publishing business, despite the early success of *Journeys* — "We are in the 'sharing Jesus business.'"

# THREE

# A MISSION

TO HELP

# SOLVE

THE

# WATER CRISIS

## MOLLY & GEORGE GREENE, III
*Charleston, South Carolina*

George and Molly Greene can rattle off every statistic related to our global water crisis, most of them quite sobering: 2,300 people die each day due to illness from inadequate drinking water, sanitation, and hygiene. Thirty-five percent of the global population lives without adequate sanitation. For children in developing countries, school attendance is reduced by the three hours necessary to go and collect water, which is usually still contaminated.

The Greenes should know about water — for 20 years, they owned an environmental consulting company based in Charleston, South Carolina, testing water and environmental samples from across the U.S. But they weren't involved in treating water. At least not until Hurricane Mitch hit Central America in 1998, devastating much of Honduras's water supply. The Greenes were familiar with Honduras from their church's mission work, hosting some Honduran children who were undergoing surgeries in the U.S., and their daughter's time teaching there after college. George learned about the devastation and the number of people impacted by the hurricane on the radio and felt like God really wanted them to respond — to do something. "So George emailed the Episcopal Bishop of Honduras, whom we had met, simply saying, 'We know a little bit about water — what can we do to help?' He didn't think it would even get to him because of infrastructure damage in Honduras from the storm," says Molly. One day later, back came the reply: "We need six water treatment systems."

With a very specific request on which to focus, the Greenes were ready to move quickly. But there was just one problem — they had never designed and built water treatment systems. After searching the internet — in 1998, not what it is today — George came to the conclusion that "Water treatment is not rocket science. Let's design our own," recalls Molly. "He sat down at the table with a yellow pad and some engineering textbooks and within a few hours he had sketched out a design and given it to another engineer to build a prototype." With help from the U.S. Air Force and the late Senator Strom Thurmond's office, six water treatment systems and 50 tons of relief supplies were delivered to Honduras. Within two weeks, 16 people from the Greenes' company were on the ground, installing water systems. "We didn't know at the time that these were in locations that had really never had clean, safe water," says George. The main water source for the region was from "the river of death," a name coined by locals who knew it was heavily contaminated and made people deathly ill.

The Greenes also didn't know that they had just created their second company, to do hands-on work — not work in a laboratory — to help address a worldwide water crisis. "We saw a world we hadn't seen before," says George, "and that's always life changing. But for a while, we looked at this new service as strictly a business opportunity. For two years, we designed and installed water treatment systems in Honduras, Turkey, El Salvador, and Mozambique, often in response to a disaster."

> "We saw a world we hadn't seen before, and that's always life changing."

The Greenes quickly realized, however, that although the market is huge — 1.8 billion people without safe water — trying to sell something to people who lack money just doesn't work for a for-profit business. It took them those first two years to figure out that their new venture needed to be mission oriented. "We were trying to do it our way," says Molly. "But it wasn't God's way. We finally saw that God was working in our lives in such a mighty way, helping us to see that our plans were not necessarily His plans, and that we needed to seek Him, trust Him, and that He would help us figure out how to move forward."

Molly was particularly captivated with what she read in a book called *Halftime*, by Bob Buford, which addresses how people can move from success to significance in their second half of life. After George read the book, he told Molly they needed to set aside a time to pray and to come to their own meeting of the minds. "We spent that day trying to discern God's guidance and seeking direction for our lives," says George. "We knew we wanted a change from our environmental business, which had become very focused on the federal government, rather than industry and individuals. Our business was far more successful than we ever dreamed, and as we look back now, we believe that God used our business to enable us to do what we're doing today. We knew the Lord was calling us to focus on the water crisis."

In 2001, the Greenes sold their company and started Water Mission, a non-profit Christian engineering ministry providing sustainable, safe water solutions to people in developing countries and disasters. Water Mission has about 50 employees in Charleston, augmented by numerous volunteers, and another 200 full-time staff in nine countries: Haiti, Honduras, Mexico, Peru, Malawi, Uganda, Kenya, Tanzania, and Indonesia. The Greenes learned through trial and error that employing indigenous staff in the countries in which they operate is critical.

"There's a very high failure rate for our type of work, primarily because it often creates dependencies and sends a message that people in these countries are incapable of helping themselves," says George. "Local staff understand the culture and how best to work in these rural villages. We certainly train them on the technical part. The harder part is what we call community development, making a long-term investment in the people and the community. That includes education — in many cases, people don't even know that dirty water can make them sick. These opportunities are when the real hard work takes place, but they're also the most rewarding, because they're where relationships are built and the Gospel is shared. The local staff members are our hands and feet in this effort. We're providing the engineering expertise and the funding to support our operations, but they are making these long-term relationships happen."

As of 2016, Water Mission has completed over 2,000 projects in 52 countries, and has helped more than three million people have clean water. Water Mission takes a comprehensive approach to the crisis with water, sanitation, and hygiene — or WASH, for short. About 150 projects are completed each year, with another 600 in various stages of completion. Each community managed project can take anywhere from 18 months to two to three years. Water Mission also helps in emergency situations — in the past few years they've responded to flooding in Malawi, a typhoon in the Philippines, massive refugee settlements in Tanzania and Uganda, an earthquake in Nepal, and the Ebola crisis in Liberia. After a disaster, people die faster from lack of water than from anything else. The mission is to get water to the people as quickly as possible, meaning within days. Often Water Mission's disaster-response projects transition into community development projects.

"We're encouraged by what we've been able to accomplish with the prayers and support of so many, but we know we're only scratching the surface of the need," says Molly. "Still, each project serves, on average, 2,000 to 3,000 people. We do believe we're transforming lives in multiple ways. Safe water for now and the 'Living Water' for eternity!"

# FOUR

# DRAWING
### A
# LINE
### IN THE
# SAND

## LINDA & STEVE
*Indianapolis, Indiana*

What if you gave away more money than you ever anticipated? What if you actually gave away more than you kept?

For some people, giving is itself a natural gift, embedded in their DNA. For others, like Steve and Linda, it's a joy that was only discovered after some hard truths — about money and its purpose, materialism, and the journey not to just find Jesus, but to live a life as a disciple for His kingdom and not the world's.

Steve achieved financial success at a young age in his career and life. With an income approaching seven figures and a very comfortable lifestyle, he thought everything was "pretty well set." And when he went into his first planning meeting with his advisor, he assumed he would hear that he was on cruise control as far as future financial security. That wasn't the case. The short story is that after learning how much he'd have to continue making to fund his current lifestyle and future retirement, Steve had an epiphany, suddenly realizing that "enough is never enough."

> "The truly free man is not the man who has everything in the world, but the man who needs nothing from the world."

"When I left the meeting, I went and prayed for several hours," says Steve. "Linda and I knew that we needed to go in the opposite direction. I kept thinking about a quote I liked: 'The truly free man is not the man who has everything in the world, but the man who needs nothing from the world.' I was trying to get 'enough' for security, but what I needed to do was refocus so that I didn't need so much. It was the way to real freedom — especially from fears and anxiety about 'enough.'"

Steve and Linda drew their line in the sand: Everything above a certain lifestyle line would be given away. The couple actually wrote a covenant with God. They realized that there could be years they might struggle and they debated what that would mean to their giving covenant. But they also realized that if they didn't fully commit to a line, their line would keep rising. As Steve remembers it, "If that happened, we would never give what God intends for us to give. At that critical point in our lives, our passion for giving began."

The couple soon experienced what long-time givers know — the joy of giving money away far outweighs the joy of spending it on material goods. But suddenly, they did face a challenge, one they had considered when they wrote their covenant. Within 90 days of creating their covenant, Steve's business suffered a setback when a major customer decided to phase out its business with Steve. The big question was: How would this affect their giving plans?

"Everything had suddenly changed," says Steve. "But we know that everything might always change. We stuck with our plan — and, amazingly, I had some very big and very positive changes with my business. In a few short years, we were giving away three times what we said we were going to. That wasn't what we pictured happening." Even during subsequent challenging times — such as the recession of 2008-2009 — they maintained their generous giving. Says Steve, "All I can say is that God has been faithful to us every step of the way."

In 2012, their giving took a different turn, and all because of a deceased newborn baby found in a dumpster. Moved and saddened by the fact that the child was a "Baby Doe," Linda felt compelled to act. She contacted the coroner, inquiring about what would happen to the baby. When she learned that without someone coming forward the baby would be buried in a mass, unmarked grave, Linda felt like God said, "No." She asked to adopt the baby in death and give it a name and a proper burial.

A new ministry was born. He Knows Your Name Ministry exists to honor every child with a name in life and dignity and honor in death, helping women and families say goodbye to children with burials, services, and headstones, including for aborted or miscarried babies. She's also adopted a dozen nameless and abandoned babies in death, giving them the names they deserve.

Linda's ministry began to blossom and it brought the couple to an epiphany. Meeting with their lawyer to set up a new 501(c)(3) organization for He Knows Your Name, the couple was given a full accounting of how much money they had already given away. They didn't really know — and were staggered at the amount.

"We never would have guessed that we even had that much money to give away," says Steve. "I also realized how much that money would have grown had we kept it and invested it. So we sat down at our kitchen table and asked ourselves three important questions. Number 1: If we had known at the beginning that we were going to give away this much money, would we have signed on? The answer was no, because the number would have frightened us. Number 2: Would we do this again? The answer was yes, without a doubt. Number 3: If this money was put back into our bank account tomorrow, what would we do with it? How would it change our lives? In other words, what have we missed out on? Our answer was that we've missed out on nothing. With tears of joy we were overwhelmed with the thought of what we would have missed had we not given."

That conversation left Steve and Linda asking the next question: How much more can we give? The answer to that question was that the couple committed to their first seven-figure gift, to an organization doing worldwide church planting with a strong focus on disciple building. "We don't think of ourselves as people who can give a gift of that size easily," says Steve, "but we felt led by God and His faithfulness to us."

Steve and Linda are intentional givers, evaluating their gifts using various criteria. Their biggest gifts are reserved for those organizations with which they have a personal connection. One of those takes Steve to a remote area of the Ukraine three to four times a year where he serves as a pastor for a small ministry spreading the light of the Gospel there.

An unexpected, and very emotional, bonus for Steve and Linda has been learning of the giving of their four children.

"When they were old enough to appreciate it, we shared with them our history of giving and some of our larger gifts and the reasons why," says Steve. "It was one of the sweetest moments we've ever had with our children. We've since learned that our kids give very generously to their own passions and causes — they don't have as much to give, but we think they give more freely than we do. We've heard story after story of what they've done, which has amazed and challenged us even more."

# FIVE

# WHO EXPECTS
### TO GO TO THE
# DENTIST
### AND COME OUT WITH A
# STACK OF CLOTHES?

**KERI & BRENT MILLER**
*Auburn, Alabama*

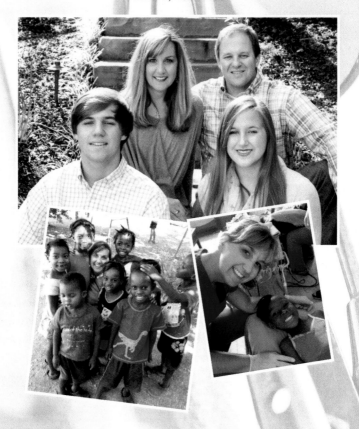

The small college town of Auburn, Alabama is home to dentist Keri Miller, her husband Brent, and their two children. It's also in the middle of a rural area where the need for access to dental care is great, but the need for the basics is often even greater. Sometimes it's food, or Christmas gifts, or new clothes for children to wear to school. And sometimes it's simply the need to have a "good shepherd."

When Keri went into practice as a pediatric dentist in 2002, she didn't envision a practice on one side of a building and a ministry on the other — her ministry, which is what she considers her interaction with her young lower-income patients, mostly on Medicaid. The original practice she joined treated patients from an affluent part of Montgomery, but when she and Brent moved to Auburn and bought a satellite practice they were able to dedicate half of it to serving low-income patients. "It really opened my eyes to people — and needs — from whom I'd been shielded," says Keri.

> "Lighthouse Children's Dentistry is a place where we have the opportunity to love on these kids."

As that part of the practice, which Keri named Lighthouse Children's Dentistry, grew, Keri hired two other dentists to help her with the workload. But Lighthouse is so much more than a practice split from her other one by a building's wall and a level of income. Put simply, "It's a place where we have the opportunity to love on these kids," says Keri. "Many of them are in foster homes; some are from the Alabama Sheriff's Girls Ranch nearby. "Often they are living in true poverty. And very often their parents, grandparents, or foster parents need support and guidance in their roles. If children are removed from a parent's home, sometimes they go to grandparents, who often aren't prepared on short notice to have young children join them. After we saw enough of these situations to know the needs were so great, we began collecting clothes, shoes and food and set up a type of 'clothes closet' in the practice so we can offer them what they need. Other times we anonymously mail families things they need. But it's not just about 'things.' It's often about shepherding adults into what we hope are better situations. Sometimes parents just need a little help with knowing how to care for their kids."

A natural outgrowth of her work with needy children in Alabama is Keri's work with two groups in Haiti. "I'm not even sure why I signed up for my first trip to Haiti," says Keri. "I went with a group to provide dental care to patients at the Christian Light School in Port Au Prince, Haiti. For one reason or another I keep feeling called back."

Christian Light School was founded in 2000 by a retired teacher from Florida and provides education, textbooks, uniforms, school supplies, two meals a day and medical and dental care to its more than 260 children. Keri also provides dental care through Have Faith Haiti Mission, one of the non-profit groups operated by author Mitch Albom's A Hole in the Roof Foundation. Children at Have Faith are cared for medically, nutritionally, educationally and spiritually, and are taught in both French and English, with the goal of helping them achieve a high school diploma.

A couple of months after a trip to Have Faith, Keri received a call that one of the children had broken several teeth badly and the local dentist believed she needed either a root canal or the teeth extracted. Keri said she would come back and take care of it. "I had to consult with a friend on how to do this root canal in a remote setting without all of the necessary equipment. This friend offered me a dental unit that was no longer being used and somehow, despite all odds, I was able to get that unit into Haiti. When I saw the child, I couldn't believe my eyes — she really only needed a filling, nothing more complicated. But if I'd known that before I went, I would never have been able to get a dental unit for them. In fact, I don't know if I ever would have gone back to Haiti." Since that visit, Keri has gone several more times, taking more dentists with her. On one trip, she had the opportunity to go to another school, in a remote area up in the mountains — "Nothing more than a shelter, really, with no water or electricity," says Keri. "But we were able to provide dental care nonetheless."

And that's where her husband, Brent, comes in. Brent has been on numerous mission trips over the years, to Guatemala, Uganda, the Dominican Republic, and Haiti. His passion is water — specifically, the lack of clean water for so many in impoverished areas. Several years ago, Brent did a "water catch" at Christian Light School and has returned to Haiti to help come up with solutions for those living in the mountainside shelter. A "water catch" is exactly as it sounds — a gutter, a down spout and a 50 gallon drum to catch rain water during the rainy season. It's not fancy or complicated, but it's water.

On a trip Brent took to Uganda with Living Water International, the mission was several-fold: teach good old-fashioned American baseball, witness to the love of Christ, and catch some water.

"Uganda is predominantly a soccer country, but the kids had just recently been introduced to baseball," says Brent. "So we decided to use baseball as a ministry tool. We would show up in the morning and see a couple of hundred kids waiting for us. They were an easy audience to witness to before we started teaching them about baseball. In the afternoons, we put in water catch systems at houses and helped the villagers carry their water buckets home from the well. Most of the people in this village have to walk anywhere from one-half mile to a mile round trip to get water from a well, carrying a five-gallon bucket that weighs 40 pounds when full."

On one trip to the well, Brent and his group noticed a woman who had been sitting silently. A translator told the group she had been listening as they talked to others about Jesus. She wanted to know more. "After about 10 minutes, she asked to be a part of His kingdom, too," says Brent. "The last thing she said to us before we left is that she didn't know if she'd be alive the next day. She said that she might be killed if people found out that she had converted to Christianity in the mostly non-Christian area. That was a profound moment."

The Millers have taken their children on a number of trips — it's very important to them that their kids experience other parts of the world "outside our American bubble." But both Keri and Brent stress that none of them are special: "We're just a normal family, but we have been intentional about making ourselves available for God's work. All you have to do is be open to being used wherever you are planted. Sometimes what we've been asked to do seemed crazy at the time, but we learned that when you just say 'okay' to the little steps, more opportunities come. It doesn't take a special skill, it just takes being available."

# SIX

# A GOD JAR,
# A SON'S HEART,
# A LEGACY

---

**SHERRY & DAVID LARSON**
*Milwaukee, Wisconsin*

H ow much difference can a mere $600 possibly make in the world?

For Sherry and David Larson, and for thousands of people who felt the touch of their son, Brad, $600 in a "God jar" is a symbol of a son's heart and of a sweet legacy that revolves around selfless giving.

{ What they discovered about their son after the accident led them to think differently about what's in the heart of a pure giver. }

Bradley "Brad" Jesse Larson was only 22 when he was killed in an automobile accident on an interstate near Indianapolis, Indiana in April 2006. Just weeks away from his graduation from Taylor University and planning to attend law school at the University of Wisconsin, Brad and four others died on their way back to school after setting up for a banquet to honor the university's new president. The Larsons had always been "willing givers," but what they discovered about their son after the accident led them to think differently about what's in the heart of a pure giver.

It wasn't just the $600 they found in Brad's "God jar," although that touched and moved them. "When our children were growing up, we asked them to save 10% of every dollar they earned and give another 10% to God," says Sherry. "We found Brad's God jar and savings jar from his childhood. They were just little glass artichoke jars labeled with masking tape. The savings jar was empty, which made us laugh, but the God Jar was filled with $20 and $50 bills stuffed in it totaling more than $600. That was especially precious for us to find and we knew it was meaningful to him — especially after we received notes from friends about his generous giving."

The Larsons read, and saved, every one of the hundreds of notes and cards that came to them after Brad's death. One in particular opened their eyes into Brad's giving heart. The note, from a high school classmate who the Larsons didn't know, recounted how Brad had given her some money for a mission trip: "I was constantly in the halls trying to sell candy bars and everything under the sun. One day during this time, Brad approached me with a card. Inside was $100 and a very thoughtful and encouraging note. He said this was his tithe money and he wanted to put it toward something he knew would do God's work. I have never forgotten what Brad did. I want to thank you for raising such a thoughtful, God-fearing son. His life blessed my life."

> "He said this was his
> tithe money and he wanted
> to put it toward something
> he knew would do
> God's work."

The Larsons knew of some of Brad's giving — "Much to my dismay, Brad would put cash in the mail to a charity or cause he was interested in donating to," says David. "He always said 'I don't want or need a receipt; I just want to make this contribution now.' Brad never had a job during the school year while in high school, so for him to give $100 to a classmate raising money for her mission trip was a lot of money and a very significant gesture."

David and Sherry also discovered more about the inner workings of their son's heart, almost by accident. About four months after the accident, Sherry noticed some spiral-bound notebooks on the floor of Brad's closet at home and assumed they were notebooks he'd used in his college classes. But they were journals that Brad had been keeping since his junior year of high school, with the last entry a week before he died.

Included in the journal were letters he had sent to Sherry and David. Although first written as journal entries, Brad actually mailed the letters to his parents. In his first one, he wrote, "I know you guys have a lot of wisdom and knowledge and that is something that I would love for you to share with me. My idea is that I ask you questions about a variety of topics and you answer them separately, not collectively. Both of your thoughts and opinions could differ drastically on certain issues. I think this could best be accomplished in letters — mostly for my benefit. The letters would give me something tangible that I could always keep and treasure.

Instead of Brad treasuring these letters, the Larsons now keep and treasure Brad's writings — they collected all of his journal entries and published them in a book, *Brad's Legacy: A Son's Heart Discovered* and donated hundreds of copies to people they thought would be interested in reading Brad's entries. The Larsons were particularly taken with an early letter from Brad asking, "Do you have anything that you would like to share with me regarding financial matters?" In it, Brad recounts how much a recent Bible study helped him learn about financial carelessness and being a steward for God. Unlike many his age, he even suggested that his parents stop sending him an allowance and stop paying for so many of his routine expenses.

Also included in the book are entries from a prayer journal — "Rich with so many wonderful insights and deeply moving prayers," says David. "We included everything from his inner spiritual life. Nobody had ever read these journals — we didn't even know they existed."

Although the Larsons, like any parents who experience the sudden, tragic, and devastating loss of a child, grieved immensely and for many years for their son, they take comfort in their firm belief that God inspired Brad to write with such insight and introspection into life, generosity, family relationships, and faith.

"His words are a gift to us," says David. "We came to know Brad better in his death than we ever could have known him in life."

# SEVEN

A STAR

# ATHLETE

SHIFTS TO

# "LITTLE ME —
# BIG WORLD"

**JAIME GARCIA**
*Pharr, Texas*

# M

oney, admiration, professional recognition, a comfortable home.

Major League Baseball pitcher Jaime Garcia has come a long way indeed, from the poverty and drug-driven violence of his native Reynosa, Mexico, an industrial border town on the south bank of the Rio Grande River. His journey back to Reynosa — to give back in a way that goes beyond writing a sizable check — has been a long one. It all finally came together for Jaime when his financial advisor offered him a piece of advice after introducing him to a community development organization that gives Mexican residents the chance to earn houses through community service. The advice? Don't just give — Go. Own the project. Suddenly, "big me — little world" became "little me — big world."

> Don't just give — Go.
> Own the project. Suddenly,
> "big me — little world"
> became "little me —
> big world."

Jaime, a high-profile success story of Reynosa, left his hometown with his family when he was just entering high school, settling in Mission, Texas. Eventually, he caught the eye of the St. Louis Cardinals, who drafted him in the 22nd round of the 2005 Major League Baseball draft. Finally making it to the big leagues in 2010, Jaime was third in voting for Rookie of the Year and began the 2011 season as the team's number three starter. That same year, he signed a four-year extension with the Cardinals, including options for the following two seasons — a development that could see him earning $50 million over six years.

But his professional life was not without pain — literally. He's had, and recovered from, three arm surgeries. "I've gone through pretty much anything you can go through as far as physical pain and surgeries and rehabs," says Jaime. Raised a Catholic, Jaime's faith has always been important to him and is the one thing he could rely on while going through so many physical challenges in his career. During a period of rehabilitation down-time in 2013-14, Jaime began talking to teammate Adam Wainwright about the work Wainwright was doing to help the underprivileged. Wainwright had for years been Jaime's spiritual mentor.

Jaime shared with him his long-time vision for going back and helping improve Reynosa — homes to build, schools to open, children who need help escaping the cycle of poverty.

It was about that time that Jaime's financial advisor connected him with 1 Mission, an Arizona-based community development organization. Hundreds of miles away, Alicia and Francisco, a young couple in desperate straits in Caborca, Mexico, had also been connected to 1 Mission. Trying to survive in a barrio in a home built from cardboard and other scraps, the couple began the process of completing the community service hours necessary to earn their own home, which they eventually learned had been paid for through the charitable organization. In 2014, when Alicia and Francisco finally got their home, Jaime funded 25% of the 101 homes 1 Mission built for families in Puerto Penasco, where Alicia and Francisco's new home was. Eventually heeding his advisor's advice to go, Jaime temporarily halted his rehab to travel to Mexico and helped build one of the houses.

> "I didn't even think about baseball. It's an experience that definitely changed my life and touched my heart."

"I was a little worried about taking a break from the training at first because I like to have my routine and do things the way they should be done," says Jaime, who had undergone thoracic outlet surgery the previous July. "But when I was there, I didn't even think about baseball. It's an experience that definitely changed my life and touched my heart."

Jaime's return to Mexico reminded him of the poverty he left behind and had almost forgotten. He met people like Hector and Silvia Peña, who'd moved into a new 11-by-22-foot home Jaime helped to build during his visit. Standing beside others who were gaining the service hours that would eventually earn them a home of their own, Jaime helped with each phase of the three-day build — one day to lay the foundation, another to erect the walls and lay the first layer of stucco, and the last to finish the roofing, stucco and installation of doors and windows. Moved by the experience, Jaime returned to the states and began to make plans for how to help his hometown of Reynosa.

A "chance" meeting with a stranger in a chiropractor's office put him in touch with Strategic Alliance, a Texas-based ministry that connects teams and individuals to help the hurting people of Mexico in practical ways. Several months later, Jaime returned to Reynosa and was moved by the incredible needs that still existed there. Jaime told the founder of Strategic Alliance that he would cover the cost of 25 new houses in Reynosa. He joined in to build one and also covered the cost for tuition, supplies, and uniforms for 119 school children. On the second day, Garcia headed to his old Little League field, where he threw a party for area baseball teams and passed out merchandise and equipment. He describes it as the highlight of his trip. "I remember being there and dreaming about being a baseball player," Jaime says. "And I remember always thinking how cool it would be to just meet somebody, touch somebody who's played in the big leagues. I know a lot of those kids look up to me, so to be able to hang out and spend quality time with them is something I really make a priority."

Jaime still plans to focus on shelter and schooling in Reynosa, but after his trip he also partnered with Water Mission to fund a project in Mexico that will bring clean water to approximately 10,000 people.

"I always dreamed of going back and spending a lot of time with kids, to teach them and show them that there are a lot of great things they can accomplish from doing things the right way," Jaime says. "It doesn't have to be the biggest or greatest town in Mexico. But I want to be able to use my name and make a big impact in the community, more than I've done. To give them hope is something I've always had in my heart."

# EIGHT

# LET THE
# CHILDREN COME
# TO THEM

## MOLLY & TOM ARMSTRONG
*Charlotte, North Carolina*

T he Scripture verse Matthew 13:12 could sum up the past 30+ years for Tom and Molly Armstrong: For to the one who has, more will be given, and he will have an abundance . . .

Most people would say, "Are they crazy?" But the Armstrongs say, quite simply and very convincingly, "The Lord brought them to us. He's always helped us work it out." In addition to the horses, cow, llamas, and a camel on their farm outside Charlotte, North Carolina, the Armstrongs have 15 children, 8 boys and 7 girls, half of them mixed-race — all adopted. Now ages 14 to 38, their abundance of children at home is winding down. "We're getting to the end, so we're sad," says Molly.

$$\left[ \text{ “The Lord brought them to us. He's always helped us work it out.” } \right\}$$

It all started back in 1978 after Tom finished dental school at Washington University in St. Louis and the couple moved to North Carolina so Tom could open his first practice. They had decided when they were first married that they wouldn't have children unless they could adopt. "It was just a personal decision we made," says Tom. "We weren't Christians at the time we married, so I can't say it was because of anything the Lord said to us."

They eventually did become Christians, just about the time they were finishing dental school, and that's when the Lord went to work on them.

One evening while Tom was still working on patients and Molly was at the receptionist desk, Molly had a call from a patient who asked if they wanted to come get a four-month old baby boy — right then. Tom told Molly to tell the woman they'd come as soon as he finished with his patient. When they picked up the baby, the Armstrongs put him in a bassinet in the back seat of their Volkswagen Bug and headed to a pharmacy to pick up some formula and diapers. "We had no idea what we were doing," says Tom. The next day they learned he had a double ear infection and several other infections throughout his body. "That was our beginning of parenthood," Molly remembers.

They got a second baby boy — and then the abundance really began. The Armstrongs then took in siblings ages 3, 4, and 9, removed from a foster home where they had been for three years. After another child joined them soon after, they were parents of six children — a "challenging group of kids," recalls Tom, because of the hard situations they came out of. We cried a lot, but we just said, 'Lord, you work it out.' We were also still open to receiving other children. One time there was a group of six that we tried to get, but we couldn't."

The Armstrongs kept adding to their family, another time getting two boys in the same way that they got their first child: with an urgent phone call and a pick-up the same day. At one point they had 14 children at home, adding on to their house year after year and finally buying a 22-passenger bus as their family car. Tom had a contractor custom build a round dining table — "the biggest table we could get in the house through double doors." Shopping for groceries when there were 14 at home meant a trip to a Sam's Wholesale Club about every three to four months to fill up a trailer. Parenting that many children depended on one key word: logistics. "Oh and rules, of course," says Tom. "We kept track of everybody and what was going on. The children took care of our animals on the farm and had to do chores, for which they got an allowance as they got older. Bedtime was a specific time so that Molly and I had a chance to say hello to each other at the end of the day."

The Armstrongs spent the weekends playing with the children and always made time to create special memories. They traveled to the beach every year and visited Disney World every four or five years. Several years ago they did a western tour — 10,000 miles on the bus. Molly recalls, "We saw all the parks and the Pacific Ocean and just had a good old time."

When the Armstrongs had only their first two boys, they felt the Lord encourage them to homeschool the children. It made sense as both boys were having a difficult time in school — one strongly rebelling against homework and the other so gregarious and fun-loving that he just wasn't interested in focusing on school. The beauty of homeschooling, say the Armstrongs, is that parents alone decide how to customize the work to fit their children's needs. Tom Says, "I wanted to see them doing something they really liked when they grew up, perhaps in their own businesses. So they would spend two or three hours doing schoolwork and then something like helping to build a house or working with our farm animals. I always told our kids that if they went to college it should be for an interest that prepared them for something they really wanted to do."

The Armstrongs' heart for their children included making each child feel special on Christmas mornings. When they had 14 children at home, Tom and Molly knew they needed a creative way to keep their kids' presents organized. Thus was born "the box." It was the GI Joe era and thus everything was very small so instead of wrapping each of those 50 small things for each child Tom and Molly would combine them all in one box for each child and wrap it. They used tape to make a 3-foot by 5-foot square for each child to sit in and open their presents. "It was total chaos," says Molly, "but sitting in their own 'square' gave each child the feeling that what they received was really theirs."

Tom and Molly have made an impact on others by talking about and encouraging adoption. "There are many different ways you can adopt children if you're willing to have an open mind," says Tom. "We counsel people on keeping their hearts open, like we did. We just always said, 'Thank you, Lord. We've had a great life, we enjoy our kids, send us more if you want to.'"

As of 2016, the Armstrongs are now grandparents but still have six of their children at home. "It's really quiet here now," says Tom. "Nothing to it anymore."

# NINE

# A MISSION TO
# PREVENT MORE ORPHANS

**ROBIN & WAYNE HOOVER**
*Atlanta, Georgia*

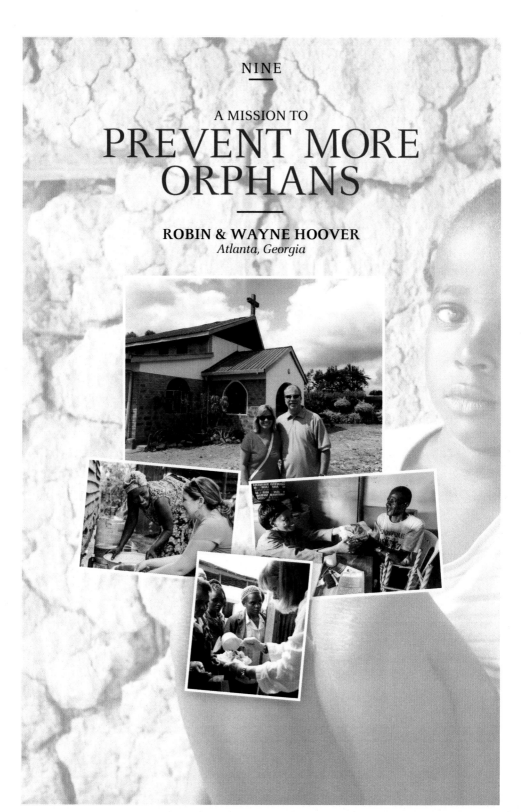

Why not prevent children from becoming orphans instead of building another orphanage?

Anyone involved in the global HIV and AIDS epidemic knows that it is no simple task. According to the U.S. Agency for International Development, during the 30 years of the HIV epidemic, an estimated 17 million children have lost one or both parents due to AIDS, with 90% of those in sub-Saharan Africa. In many respects, HIV prevention is orphan prevention.

Orphan prevention in Kenya is the goal of the organization so close to the hearts of Wayne and Robin Hoover of Atlanta. The Hoovers and others involved with the Atlanta-based nonprofit CARE for AIDS live the organization's mission: mobilize the church to care, both physically and spiritually, for families affected by HIV/AIDS in Kenya in order to prevent more children from being orphaned.

{ "We wanted to actually experience the ministry on the ground in Kenya." }

Before they experienced hands-on work with CARE for AIDS, the Hoovers were simply admirers of the organization and its founder, a young man whose family they knew. "We watched Justin Miller grow up and knew that whatever he was involved in he'd be doing a great job at it," says Robin. "After Justin founded CARE for AIDS, we began talking with him about it, learning more and more, and supporting it financially. So we started out just giving to the ministry and praying for it. Our interest grew and grew and at some point we decided we needed our own 'story' with CARE for AIDS. We wanted to actually experience the ministry on the ground in Kenya."

The Hoovers finally got their chance in 2014, spending 10 days with the organization in Kenya. They were hooked. "After you go, you just can't not be a part of it," says Wayne.

CARE for AIDS created an innovative model of care that engages local leaders, churches and communities in caring for families affected by HIV/AIDS. It's a model of care that addresses complex needs of body and soul. CARE for AIDS operates 33 centers in multiple communities throughout Kenya, and each center is located within a local Kenyan church. Each center has two counselors who guide classes of 80 HIV-positive clients through a nine-month program. Throughout the program these clients experience transformation in five key areas: physical, emotional, social, economic, and spiritual.

"Their model was born out of Justin's trip to Kenya as a college student, during which he got a sense of how many orphans there really are," says Robin. "He eventually partnered with two Kenyans who have such a heart for trying to improve things because, as they told Justin, 'There aren't enough people to take care of the children who are being orphaned.' The clients go through a program that has them come to the center a couple of times a week and they get nutritious food, job training, and a lot of counseling on how to take care of themselves and their families. They've now graduated over 7,000 clients from this program and believe they've prevented more than 20,000 children from becoming orphans."

CARE for AIDS's goal is to keep families together by helping parents learn to take care of themselves. "Once they're educated, many men and women can live healthy, well-functioning, long lives," says Robin. "There is certainly a need to build orphanages in Kenya, but CARE for AIDS aims at the root cause of the orphan problem — preventing mothers and fathers from dying." Central to CARE for AIDS's philosophy is that they always partner with a local church — "There is only one American on staff there," says Wayne. "This is about Kenyans helping other Kenyans."

> CARE for AIDS's goal is to keep families together by helping parents learn to take care of themselves.

In Kenya, the Hoovers realized what people living with HIV/AIDS regularly experience. "When people in a village find out somebody is HIV-positive, that person is totally shunned because people just aren't educated about the spread of HIV. We go into their homes and spend time with them and it's really a bright light, not just for them but for their community. The others in the village see that we are fine with going into an HIV-positive person's home — and we're also Christians and talk about the love of the Lord — and they see that we're not afraid. This has made a huge difference," says Wayne. "The homes are nothing like what we have in the U.S. — they are often simply sectioned-off corrugated metal spaces. Very few have electricity; many of the people are desperately poor."

"But they're very proud of their homes and the fact they're taking care of their children," says Robin. "They have such joy and pride in the lives they're building. It has certainly brought home to us that we often base our joy on 'things,' and theirs is built around the joy of a functioning family and the ability to be productive." Because the centers also teach skills, many of the people in the program are now able to make things they can sell to help support their families — some are even making jewelry and purses out of discarded plastic bags.

The couple says that a graduation ceremony is always a highlight. "It's a wonderful experience. While the situation in Kenya is very sad, it's so great to see how lives are being transformed physically and spiritually."

Robin and Wayne are now heavily involved with a new initiative for CARE for AIDS — raising money for scholarships for the Kenyan employees. "Many of them want to go back to school and finish a degree or get an advanced degree," says Robin. "Often, they started a degree but had to postpone finishing it because of lack of money, so CARE for AIDS decided they'd like to offer awards each year that would be for their employees to continue their education. We had an event recently and raised about $6,000. In 2016, we believe we'll be funding five more scholarships."

The ultimate goal of every CARE for AIDS center is to close. "There are many instances where they've been able to close a center because they've met the needs of the people in a village and there are no more 'customers,'" says Wayne. "That's the most wonderful thing — to have a center close."

# TEN

# LIVING
### IN THEIR
# HEART'S PROJECT

**KATHY & CURT SMITH**

A description of the location where Curt and Kathy Smith* are deeply invested in the work they feel called to do does not paint a pretty picture. They don't walk alone in the area after dark. Some areas they don't walk in during the daytime. About 20% to 30% of the houses are boarded up. The area has one of the highest crime rates in their city. Many homes are owned by "slum lords" who don't maintain the properties. Renters move in and out of homes, often only able to pay the initial deposit and first month's rent, and then are evicted. Some residents have no water and very little food. Sometimes, residents are there one week and gone the next. One child the Smiths know was in nine homes and nine different schools between starting kindergarten and finishing second grade.

At the end of the day, the Smiths don't retreat from this area to a large, comfortable home in the safe suburbs — they also live here. And, says Curt, "We love it. It's awesome."

> They don't walk alone
> in the area after dark. Some
> areas they don't walk in
> during the daytime.

Curt and Kathy, parents of grown children, have now been involved in their inner-city ministry for more than 10 years. Originally, they did live in the suburbs, but began to realize they could have greater impact if they moved in to the area where their ministry operates. Says Kathy, "When you live with others who are 'just like you,' you read the Bible and nod your head and say 'Yes, that's true and that's true, too' but then when you confront issues of real life that others are facing, you think: 'Wow, maybe I was a little more sheltered than I thought. So how do I feel about driving somebody to the hospital who smells bad? How do I feel about living among felons?' I never thought I'd be comfortable doing that, but now I consider our neighbors some of our best friends. Sometimes it's just realizing you have to be the hands and feet of Jesus for a person asking to do laundry in your house."

The seeds of being hands and feet of Jesus started with a family mission trip to the Caribbean in 2006. "It was obvious we were supposed to go on that trip," says Kathy. "We just listened to the Holy Spirit and He spoke to us. We do that often and if we hear something we're told to do, we do it — even if it seems crazy. At

*Pseudonyms to reflect this family's wish for remaining anonymous.

the end of the trip, the leader said, 'This is great and you've all done good things. Now what are you going to do when you go home?'"

One of the Smiths' daughters had never felt like she fit in at church, but when the family returned home she accepted an invitation to help with an after school program at an inner-city church. Curt began to accompany her and eventually the Smiths found themselves there more and more "We just kept being drawn back to that neighborhood," says Kathy. "Before we knew it, we were coming to the neighborhood two or three times a week, a 30-minute trip each way from where we were living."

> They're investing in and rehabbing homes in the area, which are provided to those in need at an affordable cost.

The Smiths prayed for several years, seeking to discern whether they were being called to move to the neighborhood. They always felt the answer was no, especially since their children were still in good schools in the suburbs. But one day as Kathy was driving home, she remembers exactly where she was on the interstate, she felt God say, "You are done. I have released you from the house." As she walked into their suburban home, Curt looked at her and said, "You just need to know God released me from the house today."

The Smiths relocated to the inner-city neighborhood and became an "anchor" family for the expanding Christian community ministry, primarily because they are living in their ministry. They're investing in and rehabbing homes in the area, which are provided to those in need at an affordable cost. They've run Bible studies for youth in their garage. They have fed children who come to play on their porch in the evenings. They've shared the Gospel with single mothers and their children and they have helped support and encourage these families and their neighbors. God put it on their hearts to create a wiffle ball field. "It's just wonderful how He keeps providing," says Kathy. "People showed up and all of a sudden we had stands for the wiffle ball field and then a little shed that became our concession stand, a scorer's table and an irrigation system — certainly the only one in the neighborhood! God just keeps bringing people to do things."

And they're going to church with their neighbors, many of whom are "baby believers." "We now have an amazing group of brothers and sisters in Christ who are unlike us," says Curt. "We are from all different races and socioeconomic backgrounds and speak different languages. We're learning so much from each other."

One of the most unique things that the Smiths have planned for their inner-city neighborhood is what Curt calls the "maker space." A software engineer for his entire career, Curt also developed an interest in robotics and micro-controllers, as well as an idea for how to get neighborhood kids involved. He plans to create a space where kids can come and start with Legos, working their way up over their school years to complex robotics. He hopes to eventually partner with a philanthropic organization in their city that is training high school graduates to be software engineers, bypassing a college degree, and helping with job placement. Even though the partnership is still in "the dream phase," Curt and Kathy went ahead and purchased a house in the neighborhood, renovated it, rented the top floor to a single mother, and have plans to put the "maker space" downstairs. The Smiths have actually purchased and renovated several homes, each one of them with either a specific ministry group or specific person or family in mind. "We really didn't know that we were risk takers, but we've learned that we are," says Curt.

The Smiths are thrilled when, as recently happened, people visit the neighborhood and "catch the vision for it." They bought a house and rented it to a couple who now lead worship at their church, but the couple feels so invested in the neighborhood that they've now bought their own house and plan to stay and raise a family there. "The best part is they're only 26 years old," says Curt. "It's so exciting to us that young people want to put down roots here."

Most of the residents in the Smiths' neighborhood have just never had a break, says Curt, nor the resources and opportunities to create better lives. "We see the reality of poverty up close, but whether we're playing wiffle ball together or delivering cookies to everybody on our block or decorating neighborhood Christmas trees or involved in rehabbing neglected homes for families in need, we're doing it together, alongside our neighbors and church family, sharing the light of Christ with each other. Kathy and I are now doing what God has put on our hearts."

# ELEVEN

EMBRACING A DREAM:
# LA FAMILIA-STYLE

**BILL LEE**
*Greenville, South Carolina*

For his first 30+ years as a working adult, Bill Lee built businesses. His career took him from selling roofing products in Alabama and Mississippi to part-ownership of a $640 million-in-revenue company to his own 10-employee consulting firm based in Greenville, South Carolina. "I always felt like I was in the right place at the right time," says Bill. That could also be said for Bill's slightly impulsive decision in 2000.

At an annual family reunion, a cousin who at the time was a Methodist minister in Chattanooga, Tennessee, asked Bill — again — when he was going to go with his church on a mission trip to Casa Hogar La Familia, an orphanage in Mexico. "I always had an excuse not to go," says Bill. "But when he asked me that year, I said, 'Where do you go and what do you do while you're down there?' Next I heard myself saying, 'I think I'll go this year.'"

During his first visit to La Familia, Bill and a group of young college students from Tennessee did glamorous and exciting things like . . . cleaning out a damaged cistern. It was hard work but he had fun with the children in the orphanage. When he decided to go back the next year, he was surprised that the children remembered him. "It was just delightful to feel like I meant something to a group of kids so far away from my home," says Bill. After his third trip to Mexico, Bill thought he had it all figured out and decided to put together a mission team from his own church. "I made a lot of mistakes and learned a lot, particularly what not to do, but I was off to the races. I decided I was going to make a serious commitment to La Familia."

He sold his company to two of his key employees, although he remained part of the consulting team, survived prostate cancer, and then turned his attention to some abandoned children in the state of Puebla, Mexico.

Originally founded by the Mennonites, the orphanage had been turned over to the direction of a Methodist church in Puebla. Methodist churches in the U.S. provided financial and hands-on support. But Bill felt the various groups didn't have a real relationship with each other — "The right hand didn't know what the left hand was doing," he says.

Bill organized a group meeting in Memphis and the representatives of each church gave themselves a name: Amigos de la Familia. Just like that, and very much like his days in the professional world, Bill became co-leader with a friend named, Marshall Sansbury. The two took an eight-day, 3,000 mile trip through Mexico together, sharing their dreams and visions for La Familia. And also just like that, Bill decided to set up Embrace the Dream, a 501(c)(3) non-profit, to get commitments from more people and organizations. "I didn't do any 'official' fundraising," says Bill. "I just told everybody I knew about La Familia and what we do there. I built a website, wrote a blog, and created a newsletter. Slowly but surely we started generating more interest."

Embrace the Dream's commitment is to teach the orphanage's children about the love of Jesus and to give them an education so they can make their own living as adults. "The children often come from backgrounds in which education is just not part of their culture," says Bill. "The area is very rural and a job working in the fields is common. We committed to paying tuition for the children eventually to go to a university or technical school and to taking care of the property and the children while they were at La Familia."

A steady stream of donations to keep their promises was only the first of many challenges Bill and his ministry partner had to overcome — "more obstacles than we ever dreamed," admits Bill. For one, the town is in a part of Mexico where nobody speaks a word of English, so Bill hired a Spanish tutor. "You can get along okay with smiles and hugs if you're there on a short-term mission trip, but to really lead and run something you have to speak Spanish."

Eventually, the two men and the church agreed they would part ways. "We had 18 months to find a place to go," recalls Bill. They found temporary quarters, which they would need for two years, in a town about an hour away — two small houses side by side, offering very cramped quarters. Land, even in the middle of nowhere, was running about $25,000 an acre — without utilities or a sewer connection. But one of the children's grandmothers went to the mayor of her own small town, Quecholac, and persuaded him to donate two acres of land. "It was just a miracle," says Bill, "as were the unexpected large donations that came out of the blue to help pay for building the new orphanage." At one point, we had finished the first floor but didn't have enough money to build the second. We needed big money, not just $500 or $1,000 but $50,000. A "chance" meeting with a friend resulted in a substantial donation, which would allow us to complete our dream for the new orphanage."

The new building, finally completed in 2014, also hosts twice-weekly church services, Pentecostal-style. "They sing for about an hour, preach for an hour and pray for about a half hour," says Bill. "You know you've been to church when you come out! The most important thing is that the children and the community are part of each other and about 160 previously unchurched people have been brought to the Lord through La Familia."

The children at La Familia are not "orphans" in the typical sense of the word. Many are simply abandoned — their parents have walked away from them or have moved very far away to find work. Bill noticed a family of five children on his first trip; four of them are still there. "Before they came to La Familia, they were living in cardboard boxes on a vacant lot," says Bill. "Workers from government agencies pick children up off the street and bring them to us, to their new home."

> "My faith has been the primary recipient of our work."

Bill has found what he believes is the right number of children — they can take up to 47 — and says if they start another orphanage it would be in a new town. "The need is certainly great, but we've found that we have an excellent and strong community with this number of children. We have 35 right now, from infants to age 21. Many of the older ones are still with us because they didn't go to school when they were younger, so we homeschool them, get them up to grade level and then they go to the local public school, from which they can graduate." Alumni of La Familia are now in universities or technical schools studying architecture, design, cosmetology, and cooking. Two beloved directors, husband and wife, and four volunteers keep the place running.

Back in Greenville, where Bill still lives and does his consulting work – he goes to La Familia six times a year — he's teaching Spanish to teachers in an inner-city Greenville school and teaching English to the mothers of the Spanish-speaking students. "It's a lot of fun for me," says Bill, "but my first love is La Familia. When I look back at what we've accomplished, my faith has been the primary recipient of our work. We know God wanted us in Puebla because we could have never made it through all of the obstacles we faced had God not been with us."

# TWELVE

# A LEGACY OF
# GIVING
### THROUGH THE
# GENERATIONS

## PEGGY & CHARLES McCREIGHT
*Sumter, South Carolina*

E ven a phone call to learn about Peggy and Charles McCreight's story as generous givers includes some of "the crew" — a son, daughter, daughter-in-law and two granddaughters. But they are only a small part of the more than 25 members of the four generations of McCreights, all who reflect the heart of the patriarch and matriarch, Charles and Peggy. They're spread from South Carolina to Texas to Colorado and range in age from infant (the 13th great-grand-child) to 89 (Charles).

The short story on the McCreights is that they have given away well over half of their net worth over the years, quietly giving to causes and charities and, as important, giving their time, expertise, and energy as mentors to hundreds of people — on life, raising children, and marriage — and to their community in Sumter, South Carolina. But in the beginning, giving away money was a difficult challenge, especially for Charles.

Charles came from humble beginnings. His father had a stroke as a young adult, so Charles had to learn the gift of hard work as a teenager. By the age of 17, he was managing four Piggly Wiggly grocery stores, then served in the Army Air Corps for two years during World War II, and went on to college and became an architect. With a successful practice underway, Charles and Peggy sought financial counsel. His reaction to words of advice from his financial advisor was skeptical: "I told Peggy, 'That man is going to take all of the money we have and just give it away.' I admit I had a bad attitude at first."

Peggy had a different reaction. An only child, Peggy's father worked incessant-ly to climb the corporate ladder and was financially successful. After her father passed away, she inherited a sizeable concentration of stock in the company where her father had worked for many years. When Peggy became a Christian and began reading the Bible, she realized that God owns it all — it's His. "I saw the 'blessing' of money in a different way — it wasn't about success, hard work, and pushing yourself," says Peggy. "I had experienced a family life where money did not necessarily make people happy, even though it's what many people believe and are looking for. So I was more ready and very open to giving money away."

Charles came around to Peggy's thinking and the more they gave away, the more their net worth actually grew. "It was," says Peggy, "proof that you can't out give

God." Over the years, the McCreights became faithful supporters of Focus on the Family, Compassion International, Sumter Crisis Pregnancy Center, and Walk Through the Bible, as well as missionaries affiliated with their church. Charles volunteered extensively in the community, at one point being named South Carolina Volunteer of the Year, and contributed pro bono architectural work to several new buildings in Sumter County. Peggy says, "Our hearts desire to give is all by the grace of God." But it's their personal touch over the years that so many recount when they talk about the generous hearts of the McCreights.

> "Our hearts desire to give is all by the grace of God."

Daughter-in-law Karen McCreight says that Peggy and Charles invest heavily in the people of their community. "Peggy has counseled an endless number of women, inviting them into her home and sharing wisdom on how to apply biblical principles to life and marriage," says Karen. "Peggy and Charles also did that for many couples. They would have young couples over to talk about how to give freely from your heart. They have influenced families in this community in ways it's hard to describe."

The McCreights' biggest gift to their children and grandchildren is not financial, says daughter Nancy. "Certainly they've been very generous to us, but they've truly modeled giving and how it has to come from the heart," she says. "They never used money to manipulate us; they always gave with no strings attached and no expectations. As believers, we know that God calls us to give and that's our heart's desire. We clearly saw that in our parents."

Son Bobby offers an additional perspective on his parents' generosity. "We were taught it could be taken away at any moment — from disaster, a business downturn, the stock market — and that we shouldn't put our value and trust in money because God truly does own it all, and we know He doesn't need our money. Our parents did stress making wise decisions and being accountable for decisions. That's something we've passed down to our own children."

The McCreights' generous hearts can now be seen in the third generation of the family. Many of the grandchildren have been active in organizations such as Young Life, including helping to raise funds for those less fortunate to be able to participate in Young Life programs. One granddaughter and her husband, who were married their senior year in college, were active in hosting dinners at their home for the Clemson University football team, and ministering to many of the team members. They continue that today as the grandson-in-law is a graduate assistant coach for Clemson's football team. Another grandson helped start a non-profit program to assist war veterans in need.

One way that the family legacy continues to be passed on is at their annual summer week at the beach. In fact, "beach week" is almost legendary among the family members and friends who have gone. For over 50 years, Charles and Peggy have hosted all of the extended family that can come. The week has certainly grown from just Charles and Peggy and their four children, now requiring four houses for about 40 people in four generations. It is a cherished time of fun, fellowship, and instilling family values. Charles gets choked up when he recalls moments such as the adults playing volleyball on the beach and the young people in the house having a Bible study. Son Bobby recalls friends in Sumter who joined the McCreight family at the beach remarking that it was the first time in their lives they experienced a daily devotional around the breakfast table — "My parents were always planting seeds in young people's hearts," Bobby says.

One year recently, the great-grandchildren set up a lemonade stand during beach week. Working in the summer heat they raised more than $60 at their lemonade stand, with the money designated to help someone less fortunate go to a summer camp. Granddaughter Ann Elizabeth holds these memories close in her heart — for her, they are symbolic of everything her grandparents stand for. "When I think of the word generosity, I automatically think of my grandparents. For them, it's not about the money; it's about the important things like investing in your family and instilling values. Giving is just the constant condition of their hearts."

# THIRTEEN

# REDEFINING
### POVERTY — AND
# CREATING
### NEW WAYS TO
# SOLVE IT

## LAUREL & FRED BLACKWELL
### *Phenix City, Alabama*

Fred and Laurel Blackwell fell in love 23 years ago discussing issues of poverty. "How unlikely is that?" asks Laurel.

Before they were even married, the Blackwells developed a curriculum, used throughout the country, to help people transition from welfare to work. But for two decades they remained in their established career paths until Laurel retired as president of Chattahoochee Valley Community College and Fred retired from a career in human resources and governmental affairs. They didn't have specific retirement plans in mind, but according to the Blackwells, God did.

"For three days after we both retired, we sat around and prayed — 'Okay, Lord, what can we do?'" says Fred. "Then the phone rang, and that's the last thing we remember from our 'retirement.'"

Their primary focus today came from one of those phone calls. Somebody from the Alabama-West Florida Conference of the United Methodist Church called and said they were working on a new poverty initiative and that they were told they should call the Blackwells. "They had no clear pathway for the initiative," says Laurel. "But when they asked if we were interested, we said 'Yes, we want to learn more.'"

The Communities of Transformation (COT) ministry, founded by the Alabama-West Florida Conference of the United Methodist Church, has captured their hearts, consumed almost all of their time, and given them a new passion and purpose: to help break the cycle of poverty in ways that go far beyond just providing money, meals, or clothes. The primary goal of COT is to move families toward self-sufficiency and away from instability, isolation, and dependence. COT is designed to transform lives through the building of intentional relationships across socioeconomic, cultural, and racial lines. Employment is a primary goal of COT. Surprisingly, fewer than 2% of churches across the country focus on jobs as a way to help families in poverty, yet jobs are the only way to move families toward financial self-sufficiency.

Not surprisingly, Laurel took a leadership role in COT, coordinating its six sites in Alabama, with another six sites under development. "It is a true ministry alongside the poor," says Laurel, "not *to* the poor or *for* the poor. It's a relational ministry that is very innovative and exciting. It certainly takes people off the church pews and into the ministry of healing. We think of poverty as a lack of material things. In fact, poverty as we usually define it is the least of the problems with these families. They don't have role models. They don't have relationships. They usually don't have anyone to walk alongside them to help them get to a better place."

$$\left[\begin{array}{c}\text{"We're all in poverty, it's}\\ \text{just different kinds —}\\ \text{spiritual, relational, physical."}\end{array}\right\}$$

Adds Fred, "COT is opening people's eyes to the real issues of poverty. I think we often have such a bias about people who don't have 'as much money as we do.' It's really a middle-class arrogance about how much we think we know — like, 'If other people would just be more like us they'd be happy.' In fact, in COT we don't even use the word poverty anymore. We're all in poverty, it's just different kinds — spiritual, relational, physical. People struggle with all types of deficits."

COT works with people on the margins — it could be a woman re-entering the workforce after a divorce, a person coming out of addiction treatment, or those released from prison. "They are simply people," says Laurel, "who are saying, 'I would like to get to a better place, but I don't know the path — will you help me?'"

Participants spend the first 12 weeks in a training class with their peers learning about budgeting, goal setting for themselves and their families, positive relationships and toxic ones, and exploring a new future story. Volunteers also receive an extensive 10-week training course. After training is completed, small circles of support meet regularly, assisting and nurturing the participants. This all happens around a weekly meeting, which includes dinner, child care, and positive, hope-filled experiences. In addition, the COT community identifies systemic issues that hold families back and identifies strategies to attack the barriers that plague people in poverty.

The Blackwells love that COT is also building bridges across institutions — such as local and state social service agencies — and denominations within communities. "We all have to be willing to build bridges in ways that previously didn't exist," says Fred. "When we started our work with COT, we were struck with the barriers based on labels — 'evangelical conservatives' vs. 'social justice liberals,' for example. We've figured out a way to get past that. We're all holding hands at the same table. Unlikely alliances — folks of every stripe, color, creed, and economic status — have been developed because God is in the midst of this. He is orchestrating this in every community."

Sometimes those communities really need healing. One of COT's communities is Selma, Alabama, site of the brutalities of "Bloody Sunday," the 1965 Selma to Montgomery march. "When we had our first meeting in Selma, the folks in the room that night were so excited," says Laurel. "Everybody said, 'We want to be known for more than the Edmund Pettus Bridge.' We're not only serving families who want stability for the future, we're working to facilitate healing in communities that have long been in need of it."

The Blackwells admit that one of the questions they struggled with initially was that parishioners in churches affiliated with COT would often ask, "Are you getting these people into church?" "What we discovered," says Laurel, "is that we are the church in the community. Our best story about that comes from one of our first meetings, when we were just getting started. A severely disabled African-American man simply said, 'I believe this is what the church is supposed to be.' He's exactly right, of course."

The Blackwells are also certified coaches for Spiritual Leadership, Inc., an organization based in Lexington, Kentucky, that engages former business executives to teach leaders how to apply business principles in a faith-based setting. Teams spend a year working with a church, creating a strategic ministry plan.

The Blackwells both left what they thought were their dream jobs for what they thought would be retirement, but know they have found the path God intended for them all along. "It is so extraordinary to have people from all types of backgrounds, races, faiths, education levels, neighborhoods, and socioeconomic situations working together as friends toward a common goal — thinking about a response to poverty that goes beyond 'band aids.' You can tell we're crazy about what we're doing in this wonderful opportunity God handed us. Our new work isn't just transforming other people who are walking together through COT. It is transforming us!"

# FOURTEEN

# THE
# KEY THAT TURNS
## THE
# LOCK

**PATTY BROWN**
*Pompano Beach, Florida*

If you were to receive an email from Patty Brown, she'd probably describe her most recent expedition: Shopping, as if that were something new!

Her email might even have a spreadsheet attached, showing how she tracks her purchases. Compulsive shopper? Yes. Bargain hunter? Emphatic yes. Has an excess of the same item? Absolutely yes. But Patty's intense shopping isn't for herself. She uses her shopping skills to buy flip flops, erasers, sharpeners, pencils, spiral notebooks, personal hygiene items, crayons, and toys for Operation Christmas Child shoeboxes shipped to children around the world.

> "My mission in life is to make sure we reach as many children as possible."

Patty's fire for volunteering, specifically with Operation Christmas Child, was lit in 2005 when a missionary in Guatemala spoke to Patty's church, Grace Baptist Church in Pompano Beach, Florida, about receiving a shoebox delivery. "When I heard her story, in particular that the boxes were a way to lead people to the Lord, I went a little nuts," says Patty. "I decided right then and there that I would always be a part of this ministry."

Operation Christmas Child, part of Samaritan's Purse, is the world's largest Christmas project of its kind. It uses gift-filled shoeboxes to demonstrate God's love in a tangible way to children in need around the world. Since 1993, Operation Christmas Child has delivered more than 124 million boxes to children in more than 150 countries and territories, thanks to more than 500,000 volunteers worldwide. If you donate, you can even follow your box online to discover where in the world your gift is delivered.

"I really just fell into this by hearing the speaker at our annual Missions Conference. I was unemployed at the time and I believe now that God was keeping me idle for a specific purpose. Before I knew it, I had a new job — unpaid of course — as coordinator of the Operation Christmas Child relay center in our area. My mission in life is to make sure we reach as many children as possible — to get the gifts and the Gospel to them. And within a week of taking on this project, I had a paying job too! I believe God just needed me to be 'available' to take on this new journey into Operation Christmas Child."

Patty relies on a team of like-minded volunteers, certainly necessary during National Collection Week in November, but also for shopping year-round. They start bargain hunting and buying for the next year the week after National Collection Week. It's simply a matter of her and her team watching advertisements, gathering coupons, and shopping smart — candy, for example, is marked down drastically after every major holiday. People in the community and in her church may hand her money and say 'create a shoebox for me' — "With $30, I can fill up to 10 shoeboxes from the good deals I get."

> "The purpose is to give a child a gift. And if they understand a gift, they can understand the greatest gift of all — Jesus Christ."

Patty works on the shoeboxes all year long but takes her vacation time each year in November so she can work full-time at National Collection Week. Her shoeboxes often include handmade surprises she has made from discarded items. She's used wallpaper sample books to cover old CDs and turn them into spinning tops, and she's knitted thousands of face cloths. Used greeting cards often cover the outside of the shoeboxes, turning them into decorated treasures the children can keep. Patty estimates that Grace Baptist has filled and shipped well over 15,000 boxes since 2005 when they first began.

"This is a total team effort," says Patty. "All I do is point people in the right direction. We focus on the end result: one out of three boxes goes to a child who accepts Jesus Christ. The purpose is to give a child a gift. And if they understand a gift, they can understand the greatest gift of all — Jesus Christ. The organizations that receive the boxes teach the kids to go out and make disciples. And they do. This is my favorite story: A pastor in Africa went to visit six family members of a child who had received a shoebox, which had a book in it. This was the first book this family had ever owned. He told them the story of the Gospel and asked if they would like to accept Christ as their savior. They said, 'We already did.' These shoeboxes are an amazing tool. The smallest item somebody contributes could be the key that turns the lock. We just never know how the Lord is going to use it."

Part of the reason that Patty devotes so much of her time to Operation Christmas Child is because she says she's a child at heart. "I love Christmas. I used to beg my late husband to let me leave the tree up all year because I love it so much. But this isn't about me. And the money of my own that I put into this mission isn't my tithe. This is extra gifting I just have to do. It doesn't matter to me how much I personally spend on these shoeboxes — I always have enough."

# FIFTEEN

# FROM CARING FOR
# TEETH
## AND GIVING AWAY
# EYE GLASSES
### TO
# OPENING HEARTS
## FOR THE LORD

## NITA & GAYLE CHEATWOOD
*Holtville, California*

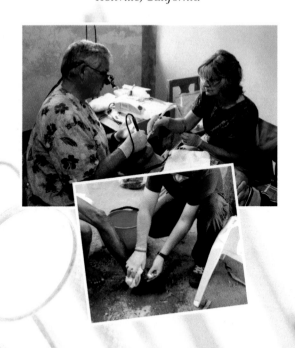

Dr. Gayle Cheatwood went on his first medical mission trip in 1974, the summer between his junior and senior year in dental school. Growing up in a California border town in the Imperial Valley, Gayle had been part of several mission trips into Mexico, just a stone's throw away. But his first mission trip to practice dentistry was to the Central African Republic — almost 9,000 miles away from his home. Since that time, he has made more than 160 trips — four each year — to 30 countries, from Brazil to Papua New Guinea, Russia, Sri Lanka, Djibouti, Vietnam, Nicaragua and the Philippines, to name a few.

> "I saw how God could use dentistry to show compassion and how we could reach people for the Lord."

"On that first trip, when I was a student, I saw how God could use dentistry to show compassion and how we could reach people for the Lord," says Gayle. "And I've just never stopped."

During that trip to the Central African Republic, Gayle practiced in a two-chair clinic in Bangui and could only do extractions because of the lack of portable equipment. Several years later, after a two-day hike deep into the Brazilian jungle, Gayle realized something had to be done so that he and other dentists could do more than just extractions in places where there was no running water or electricity.

Back home, he began experimenting with prototypes of dental equipment that would use 12-volt compressors and vacuums powered by solar panels. After he eventually had to have neck surgery because of the awkward positions in which he had to practice on patients in remote places — people sitting on tree stumps, chairs, and tables — Gayle began designing a lightweight portable dental chair. His "aha" moment was watching local farmers use corrugated plastic boxes to harvest asparagus. "I made a scale model of what I wanted and had a local box-making company, that made the asparagus boxes, create the die and do a run of 75, which I paid for myself," says Gayle. "The new chair worked and eventually we were able to improve the design and add a table, waste container, and stools. We're now on our third run of these chairs and accessories." Gayle gave the rights to the chair to the Christian Dental Society so that profits from the chairs' sales could fund scholarships for dental students on mission trips.

For 18 years, beginning in 1984, Gayle, his wife Nita, and others went to Islas Marias, a penal colony 100 miles south of Mazatlan, Mexico, in the Pacific Ocean. Although the mission was providing dental care, a simple act of sharing expanded Gayle's mission work beyond teeth. During a visit to Islas Marias, Gayle let a couple of his patients who were having difficulty seeing borrow his reading glasses — and he left them with the men. "I began taking just a few pairs of reading glasses on each trip and it eventually snowballed to us taking 800 to 1,000 pairs each trip," says Gayle. "Since that first time I left my glasses with patients, we've probably given out more than 100,000 pairs of glasses."

In 2008, Gayle set up Dental Vision Mission, a non-profit with the mission of reaching and ministering to third world people, showing compassion through dental, eye, and medical care in order to share the Gospel, and training and equipping believers to show Jesus' love by helping people with their spiritual and physical needs. Dental Vision Mission allows others to support the mission so that Gayle and his group can buy glasses and portable dental equipment. Gayle has figured out a formula for how many of each pair of glasses' strength to take on each trip — on a recent trip to Oaxaca, Mexico, the group took 2,000 pairs and handed out 1,400.

"Although we buy some, many of our glasses are donated. We were so blessed when someone donated a $7,000 piece of equipment to help with the eye care. It's really accurate and speeds things up. There are plenty of resources available — the more you get involved in missions, the more resources you discover and the more you can accomplish. Many times our older patients get very emotional because all of a sudden they're able to read their Bible, sew, or thread their fishhooks — simple things they thought they'd never be able to do again, and all because of a simple pair of eyeglasses."

Gayle likes to tell one of his favorite stories about the work his group is doing, one that took place in Tuva, a Russian republic in southern Siberia populated by nomadic tribes. A young man came to their group, frail and almost totally blind from birth, wanting to know if the ophthalmologist with the group could help him. "Unfortunately, our doctor couldn't," says Gayle. "He said, 'There's nothing we can do for your eyes but we can pray.' We got in a circle and prayed for him.

After the prayer, the local missionary was able to tell him why we prayed and he and his mother and sister accepted the Lord. Strangely, I felt a little disappointed. I thought, 'Lord, we're out here in the middle of nowhere and we prayed. Why couldn't you make him see?' Then later that night, I woke up realizing I did see a miracle. God opened the eyes of his heart. I later asked the missionary why the young man accepted the Lord. She said that, growing up in a non-Christian culture, nobody had ever prayed for them. Praying showed them our compassion and really touched their hearts."

Gayle's wife, Nita, has been on almost every trip with him — the exceptions were the ones requiring a two-day hike through the Brazilian jungle and a stay in a remote village for a couple of weeks and another trip to Guatemala that required navigating through Class III and IV rapids on the Cahabon River to get to certain villages. All of the Cheatwoods' four adult children have been on mission trips with their parents, as well as the four oldest of their 13 grandchildren. Gayle's goal is for all of them to go on a trip with him and Nita.

Gayle says that his "work," if you can call it that, is reflected in the mission statement of his non-profit organization: Following the example and commission of Jesus Christ, Dental Vision Mission exists to proclaim the Gospel in word and deed. We believe every follower of Christ is specifically gifted and prepared for some aspect of this ministry. It is our desire to bless the unreached and under-served of the world with the healing love and salvation only found in Jesus Christ. "Every trip is different and every time I'm reminded that God is in control," says Gayle. "What amazes me is how many people you can lead to the Lord just by showing them compassion."

# SIXTEEN

INTENTIONAL

# GIVING IGNITED

BY THE DIFFERENCE BETWEEN A

# DECIMAL

AND A

# COMMA

**KIM KING**
*Houston, Texas*

A life-changing meeting and a financial "oops" that changed her mindset sent retired attorney Kim King on a new "generosity walk." Invited by a local business man and friend at church to attend a Celebration of Generosity event held by Generous Giving, Kim King listened to one of the speakers talk about the three ways money can be used: as a tool, a test, and a testimony. Already inspired to increase her giving, Kim wondered how to begin. She knew she needed to be more intentional with her giving, and to do so she needed to have a better handle on her assets.

> "I began going through my old tax returns to see what { I had been giving every year and realized that although I thought I had been a pretty } generous giver, I really hadn't been."

While a corporate attorney with ExxonMobil, Kim's savings had been on auto pilot. "I was not very focused on increasing my 'standard of living,'" says Kim, "partly because I was so focused on work and just didn't spend much time shopping. I also never really focused on financial planning. Frankly, I had no idea what my net worth was and I wasn't focused on my salary some years. After the Celebration of Generosity event, I contacted a financial advisor. Following our first meeting, I began going through my old tax returns to see what I had been giving every year and realized that although I thought I had been a pretty generous giver, I really hadn't been. In the years I was blessed the most, I had given the least. I worked with my advisor to discern my own heart's passion. To that point, I had simply always been drawn to children and animals — I think because I view both of those as the most innocent and often most victimized. I decided to get a plan together and explore some organizations to give to. I knew I needed to become more focused and discern what God wanted me to do."

One of the organizations Kim began exploring is a ministry called Open Arms International, which takes in abandoned children in Eldoret, Kenya, and gives them a home in the Open Arms Village, a ministry set on 52 rural acres outside Eldoret. Open Arms' mission is to provide relief from physical, emotional, and spiritual suffering through medical expertise, education, and Christian ministry, with the vision of "Transforming Africa, One Life at a Time." Deeply moved by the stories of as many as 300,000 street children — some just babies — Kim was shocked and heartbroken. She decided to give what she considered a modest amount and then learn more about Open Arms. She sent a contribution from a philanthropic account she had set up. A few weeks later, Kim began to receive emails and calls from Open Arms' extremely grateful leaders and development representatives, thanking her for her "very generous gift." "We are dancing here in the village because of your gift," the founder told her.

"My reaction," says Kim, "was, 'Wow! That amount must go a very long way in Kenya.'"

When Kim checked with her foundation's advisor she discovered that, inadvertently, the amount sent was $250,000 — "The difference between a decimal and a comma," says Kim. "I was in shock."

> "I feel like God winked at me," says Kim. "It was Him telling me, 'This is a journey and I'm with you on it; it's going to be okay.'"

When she contacted Open Arms and explained the mistake, they insisted on returning her money. But Kim told them she needed to pray about it first. As she began pondering what to do, she remembered that after the Generous Giving conference, about two years earlier, she had made a commitment to God to give away a certain amount that year — and she hadn't done it. The incorrect amount that had been sent to Open Arms was . . . exactly the amount she failed to give. "I feel like God winked at me," says Kim. "It was Him telling me, 'This is a journey and I'm with you on it; it's going to be okay.'"

Not long after, Kim was asked to share the story at a pilot event for Women Doing Well, a Dallas-based organization that exists to inspire women to discover their purpose, ignite their passion, and develop a plan for living and giving in God's image. Kim was herself inspired by the mission of Women Doing Well. "I was really excited that they were specifically targeting women. We're professionals, entrepreneurs, inheritors — we control a lot of money. In many cases, women are widowed and have to take responsibility for the family's financial resources, even if husbands had taken the lead in the past. More and more women need to step into this role of being empowered about money."

In a heartbeat, Kim agreed to be part of an advisory board to discern God's direction for this organization. Women Doing Well Initiatives have held over 10 events for women across the U.S. with an average of 200 women coming together to learn and talk about their purpose, their passion, and a giving plan. She has been blessed with the opportunity to share her own journey and now serves on the board of directors.

Prior to getting involved with Women Doing Well, a friend suggested that Kim write a book to share her own generosity walk. "I discovered that most of the books on generosity in the Christian community are about *why* you should give," says Kim. "I felt there's a need to explore *how* to be generous — How do you make wise decisions? How do you create a giving plan? What is the woman-to-woman perspective on this?" The book, *She Speaks — The Power of Wise Stewardship —* will be released by InterVarsity Press in late 2016 or early 2017.

Kim continues to give by creating a giving plan each year and focuses on organizations that respond to the basic human desire to use their God-given abilities, to live out their purpose and care for themselves and their loved ones. "That could be microfinance programs for women who are trying to start small businesses to care for their families," she says. "It could be organizations that help women get education and better jobs. But I'm also drawn to organizations and ministries that help children, like Open Arms, and to organizations that need resources to expand or get on really solid footing. My bias is always those organizations that are intentional about sharing Christ with others."

# SEVENTEEN

# ... BUT NOW I SEE

**BETSEY & BOB RICE**
*San Antonio, Texas*

T he Bible verse 1 Samuel 12:16 says, "Now then, stand still and see this great thing the Lord is about to do before your eyes!"

For thousands of people with poor eyesight or serious eye disease who do not have access to or cannot afford health care, they are now able to fully know what the Lord has done to their eyes. Because "God working through us is what this is all about," says Bob Rice, M.D.

> "I became transformed by helping other people and decided to re-focus my life in that direction."

Bob, an ophthalmologist in San Antonio, Texas, is co-founder of I Care San Antonio, which he and a friend founded in 1993. It is a 4,000 square foot vision center at Haven for Hope, a large transitional living center for homeless people. At one time just a vision in Bob's own eyes, I Care San Antonio has six employees and 35 doctors who volunteer their time. The clinic sees about 5,000 patients a year, providing complete eye care — including exams, glasses, and surgeries — to low income and homeless children and adults in San Antonio and 10 surrounding counties. But the broader mission, according to Bob, is to carry the love of God through the hearts and skills of doctors to impoverished countries by co-sponsoring mission trips of Medical Ministry International (MMI), an organization based in Canada.

A Christian since his time in medical school, Bob joined a practice in San Antonio after leaving the Air Force in 1985. "The doctor I was working with was agnostic, but he was doing wonderful mission work with Catholic nuns," says Bob. "I realized that he was doing more work for God than I was. It motivated me to look for mission opportunities. Eventually, I was connected to MMI and began working with them in 1987. I became transformed by helping other people and decided to re-focus my life in that direction. I've now been on 24 trips with MMI."

On MMI mission trips, doctors, nurses, and other volunteers not only treat eye problems, but also provide free eyeglasses to those who need them. Finding the right pair of glasses — for patients as young as babies and toddlers to those as old as octogenarians — is no easy task, and not a matter of just rummaging through a box of eyeglasses. That's where Betsey, Bob's wife, comes in.

Pairs of glasses donated around the country are shipped to an MMI warehouse in Toronto, meticulously cataloged, and put into a database (containing about 10,000 pairs), which tells volunteer teams which types of glasses are most needed in a particular area based on past history. The glasses are then shipped to the mission sites ready to be dispensed to patients. "It can be very tedious searching through the database trying to match prescriptions to the best pair for a patient," explains Betsey. "Sometimes I think I'll never find the perfect glasses and then I go back into the database one more time and there it is!"

> Bob and Betsey firmly believe that God uses them for reasons that go well beyond medical care.

The perfect pair almost didn't happen for the tiniest of patients. On one trip to Mexico, a mother from a small village brought her three-month-old baby girl, who was born with bilateral white cataracts, to the clinic. "Her husband, the village chief, and the village doctor wanted her to take the child into the woods and let her die," says Bob. "They believed this child was possessed by 'bad spirits' because of the white cataracts. But the mother found us and we did cataract surgery on the baby. Surgery requires an intraocular lens be inserted, but at that time we weren't putting lenses in a child three months old. You can give a patient the thick-lensed cataract glasses, but they're usually adult-sized. There aren't many kids who need cataract glasses, certainly not three-month-old babies. Finding those tiny ones is next to impossible."

After 24 hours of serious praying and a lot of searching, the head optician on the trip finally located three pairs of children's glasses, each pair slightly larger so the child could grow into them. "I consider that a miracle," says Bob. "Four years later, the little girl returned. At that point, she was seeing beautifully and all she needed were larger glasses."

Both Bob and Betsey firmly believe that God uses them for reasons that go well beyond medical care. They point to numerous instances as proof. On a trip to Bolivia, a teenage boy blind in one eye because of a retinal detachment and developing one in the other eye, which would have resulted in him being totally blind, came to the team for treatment. He would need surgery from a specialist across the country in Santa Cruz. Bob's group passed the hat during dinner and immediately raised the $3,000 needed to fly the boy to Santa Cruz for the surgery.

Bob and Betsey learned that the teenager had fallen away from the church, because he just wasn't aware of God acting in his life. "But after the surgery, he gave his life to Christ because he said he now did see God working in his life — through us," says Bob. "We were very moved and it was yet another example of knowing how God is using us."

# EIGHTEEN

# A BUSINESS
## PARTNERSHIP
# WITH GOD

### STANLEY TAM
*Lima, Ohio*

S tanley Tam has lived a long and rich life giving, giving, and giving more. At age 100, it still gives him great pleasure to reflect on his "partnership" with God.

In 1936, Stanley began his path as an entrepreneur, starting a business to extract silver from photographic emulsions, but his success — or lack thereof — mirrored other companies who had tried before him. "I began praying about this business disappointment," says Tam. "God spoke right to my heart and said, 'Stanley, it doesn't need to be a disappointment. You don't need to go broke from your business. Turn it over to me and I'll make it succeed.' So I spoke back to Him, vowing that if I could succeed in business I would honor Him in every way I possibly could."

{ "I went to a lawyer and told him I wanted him to draw up documents that would make God my senior partner in the business." }

Tam started over — with $33 to his name. He traveled through 30 states, struggling for three years to make money from his business. After meeting Juanita, the woman who would become his wife, his business took a sudden turn for the better. "Juanita was my good luck charm," says Stanley. By 1940, Stanley was so happy with his business that he knew God had answered his prayers, and he decided to make good on his own promise.

"I went to a lawyer and told him I wanted him to draw up documents that would make God my senior partner in the business," says Stanley. "He just looked at me and said, 'What? You can't do that.' So I went to another attorney, who told me the same thing the first one did, but I told him I wasn't going to leave until he did something about my request. He finally understood that I meant business. The attorney incorporated my business, issued stock, and set up a foundation so that I could give 51% of my company's stock to the foundation and do His work through the foundation." Stanley's business once again began to grow, reaching $200,000 in annual revenue and then $800,000 several years later — amounts equivalent to $3 million and $10 million, respectively, today.

Then a new business opportunity crossed Stanley's path. Some of his customers wanted plastic containers for storage; others wanted containers with a faucet, spigot, and tubing. Stanley researched it all and began selling what his customers wanted, eventually establishing a second company. That company, United States Plastic Corporation, an industrial distributor of more than 32,000 types of plastic products used throughout the U.S., now has annual revenue of about $55 million. Originally set up so that his foundation owned 51% of the business, Stanley eventually heard a message from God that said He wanted 100% of the business. It happened when Stanley and his wife were in Medellín, Colombia, speaking at a church.

> "It's awfully hard to give up control of a company when you gave it birth. It's almost like a child. But obedience comes first."

"As I was speaking, something happened," recalls Stanley. "The spirit of God came upon that meeting in a very precious way. God began to talk to me, saying, 'Stanley, what's the greatest value in all the world?' As I looked at those souls in the meeting I knew the answer. The Bible says one soul is the greatest value in all the world. Then the Lord spoke to me again and said, 'Stanley, if a soul is the greatest value in all the world, would you go back to the United States and turn your entire business over to me and use the profits to spread the Gospel around the world?' I said, 'Lord, you already have 51%. Isn't that enough?' Then He spoke to me once more: 'Stanley, on the cross I paid it all for you. Now you're my disciple and I want you to do what I ask you to do. I want you to go back and turn your business over to me 100% and use the profits to spread the Gospel around the world.' You'll never know the struggle that went through me, but eventually I said, 'All right, Lord, you can have it.' It's really all about obedience to God. Many people told me that what I was doing just didn't make sense. But I felt like the Lord had showed me the way to be successful with my business and I wanted to be obedient to Him. It's awfully hard to give up control of a company when you gave it birth. It's almost like a child. But obedience comes first. That's what I was challenged with — obedience to God."

Since that decision, the foundation that owns 100% of U.S. Plastic Corporation has given about $130 million to the work of the Lord, supporting missions in third world countries.

Stanley was president of U.S. Plastic Corporation, headquartered in Lima, Ohio, for 53 years. His gift of being a smart businessman may be surpassed by his gift for evangelizing. For 83 years, U.S. Plastic has included a Gospel tract in every shipment of goods, which Stanley estimates has brought thousands of people to God. He has also spoken more than 7,000 times at churches in 30 countries around the world. His late wife, Juanita, used to say that she had seen the world through church pews.

Why has Stanley given so much? He says it's quite simple — "You don't take it with you. Money has meant less to me every year that I've lived. I just let the Lord lead me. When He asked me to do something, I said yes. It's that simple."

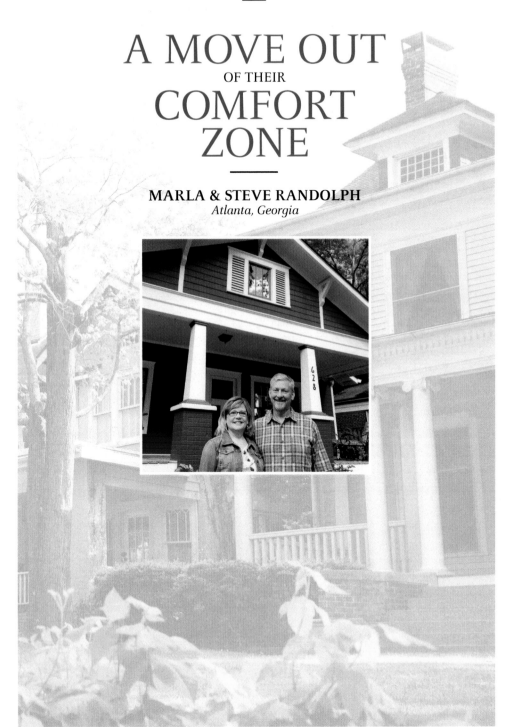

# NINETEEN

# A MOVE OUT
## OF THEIR
# COMFORT
# ZONE

**MARLA & STEVE RANDOLPH**
*Atlanta, Georgia*

"We believe that the church is first and foremost a community of people. In a word, it's formed around relationships, both with God and with one another." Those words are a key tenet of how the Village Church of East Atlanta sees itself and its mission to connect — to be in, of, and for its neighborhood.

Steve and Marla Randolph fully embrace — and live — that philosophy of their new church. It's a long way, both philosophically and geographically, from the life they once had.

{ The Randolphs started their new journey by reconfiguring their financial lives so they could live on less and live more simply by being more intentional with their money. }

When the Randolphs began to re-evaluate their life several years ago, they realized there was more to life than a comfortable existence in the typical, car-oriented, "leafy suburbs" and a big house with plenty of bedrooms and bathrooms for their two grown children and grandchildren. Initially challenged by the book *Radical: Taking Back Your Faith From the American Dream*, by David Platt, the Randolphs began a deep look into their life — committing to a new focus on paying attention to what God was putting in front of them, as well as listening to their own inner voices about dreams they had for their lives. "The book challenges Christians to step out of their comfort zones," says Steve. "That was really the idea that sparked our journey."

The Randolphs started their new journey by reconfiguring their financial lives so they could live on less and live more simply by being more intentional with their money. Increasingly dissatisfied with the lack of real connection in their suburban life, they decided to sell and move into the city, into what would feel more like a real neighborhood. "We realized we really have a heart for the city and for the challenges and joys of a diverse community," says Steve. It took Marla longer to get comfortable with the idea of selling their large house, primarily because of her vision that their children and grandchildren would have plenty of space when they came to visit. "It was a process for me," says Marla, "and God really worked on my heart. Now, though, instead of a large new home, we have one that was built in 1930 and is about half the size of our previous house. Once I let God lead me on the decision to sell and move, I haven't looked back for one second."

The Randolphs settled in East Atlanta, an area that's not quite inner-city but is certainly urban. They chose East Atlanta in part because they felt drawn to a church plant there, even though the church's membership is mostly people their children's age. The move into a very different environment required them to make a lot of adjustments. "We definitely aren't in the suburbs anymore," says Steve.

> "Our neighborhood is very economically, culturally, and racially diverse, but it has an amazing sense of community."

Just a short stroll away are tattoo parlors, coffee shops, an edible learning garden, and a Thursday afternoon farmer's market. Steve and Marla have enjoyed the new experience of walking everywhere. In fact, Marla walks to work — at the very church they were drawn to. After moving to East Atlanta, her commute to her previous job was miserable so she now works 15 hours a week at Village Church of East Atlanta. Steve, a consultant, works either at home or in a local coffee shop. The ability to walk everywhere isn't just about the quick convenience of getting to places; it's the feeling that they're truly connected to their neighborhood. "Our neighborhood is very economically, culturally, and racially diverse, but it has an amazing sense of community," says Marla. "Being here has removed travel time as a barrier to interacting with other people. That was part of our desire to be more intentional with our lives — living somewhere where the structure of the community is really supportive of developing relationships."

"Village Church has a very diverse mix of people who attend," says Steve. "Single, married, interracial couples, young people just getting started, and those getting started in new lives — possibly from homelessness, financial distress, drug abuse, even prison. It's a real smorgasbord. We want this church to be welcoming to people from any kind of background." Steve takes that goal to heart in his role as an elder for Village Church. He's heavily involved in "shepherding," providing spiritual care for some individuals and families in the church. This opportunity allows him to help address a variety of needs, whether financial, physical or spiritual sickness or re-entry into a life away from drugs and homelessness. "It's very challenging but very rewarding. We just love being an active part of the lives of our church family," says Steve.

Marla loves to disciple women and has had plenty of opportunities to do that in their new neighborhood and church. "It's very natural to develop relationships with people who are 'just like us.' Living here has opened up new relationships with people who aren't just like us," she says. "It helps us rely more heavily on God about how to be friends and how to be supportive of people."

The move to a very different area and lifestyle has led Steve to put his career and work success in the proper perspective and to grow beyond just financial giving. "God wants me to give of everything that I have," he says. "My time is what I've probably always been most stingy with, because it always seemed I had so little for myself. But I've learned that if you want to be extremely intentional about relationships and being there for people, it's so important to give your time and energy. That realization can set you on a new path of serving others with your time, energy, and financial resources. I'm still focused on my work and trying to succeed, but it's a much less important part of my life than it used to be."

Both Marla and Steve feel very much unburdened now. When they downsized, they got rid of many possessions, a process that felt really "freeing" to them. Marla even sold all of her jewelry except her wedding rings and a pair of diamond earrings Steve had given her. They don't need or want "things" — their focus now is on deep relationships with members of their church and with residents of their neighborhood, even those without faith.

"A lot of people thought we were crazy when we moved here," says Steve. "And occasionally when I'd drive home from a meeting in other parts of Atlanta and come into East Atlanta and see all the graffiti on some of the buildings, I'd think to myself, 'What in the world have we done?' But we know that God has put us on this journey. We love that our church lives by these words: Our reason for being is to be a community of people who live in light of God's redemptive story, knowing that He has loved and served us well, and calls us to love and serve our neighbors. We also know that He probably doesn't want us to get too comfortable with where we are — He may have another journey in mind for us one of these days."

TWENTY

IT ALL
# BELONGS
# TO GOD

## JEANE & GIL DE LAS ALAS
### *Chicago, Illinois*

To whom much is given, much is expected. This familiar paraphrasing is from Luke 12:48: "From everyone who has been given much, much will be demanded; and from the one who has been entrusted with much, much more will be asked."

It's a philosophy that Gil and Jeane de las Alas live by. It's also a philosophy that reminds them of their modest background, of parents who sacrificed, and of their American dream realized.

> "They taught me the importance of tithing even when finances were tight."

Both from families who emigrated from the Philippines, the de las Alases had their own period of struggle as a young married couple raising children. They made the decision that Jeane, a physical therapist, would stay home to focus on raising their children, leaving Gil as the sole breadwinner. But they drew deeply on their own upbringing. "Both of our parents instilled in us this idea of giving," says Jeane. "My parents constantly sacrificed for us six kids. We all went through Catholic school and I know that many times my parents were barely scraping by. They taught me the importance of tithing even when finances were tight. They gave wholeheartedly, even though they sometimes didn't know where the money would come from."

Adds Gil, "I try to be very reflective on the Luke passage. It really does all belong to God. We're expected to be good stewards and give to help build His kingdom."

Emulating their own parents, the de las Alases are very focused on how to impart the spirit of giving to their four young children, ranging in age from 1 to 10. They want to make sure that the children understand Gil and Jeane's humble backgrounds and the values their parents taught. "It's tough," says Gil, "especially with societal influences and because now we are able to enjoy a comfortable lifestyle. We want them to know that giving is something that can 'pay forward' for generations to come." As a way to instill the importance of giving, Gil and Jeane have the children participate in chores around the house to earn money and then encourage them to give a portion of the earnings as their tithe during Sunday School.

A few years ago as the couple began looking closely at their finances, the idea that "everything is God's — give with an open hand and He will give back to you" really resonated with them. As they were writing their long-term life and financial goals they didn't have a firm grasp on how they would reach them. Over time they wanted to give away at least 15% of their income each year. Now, because of Gil's career developments, they're planning to re-set their goals — aiming even higher.

> "Before I got a new position Jeane and I discussed that we would never 'pull back' on our giving, which meant that we would always move forward with our original giving commitment."

Gil spent 18 years at Kraft Foods on a fast career trajectory, where he ultimately was promoted to head of human resources for Kraft's U.S. commercial business. The company went through a number of changes in 2015 and Gil decided to make a career move. "I loved Kraft and they were historically a company that had supported many causes through the Kraft Foods Foundation," says Gil. "The company had a real spirit of corporate charitable giving, including encouraging employees to give with their time. That was very important to me and I knew I would feel the same way when evaluating a new job."

His departure from his long-time employer wasn't without uncertainty and stress. "My career, and what would come next, was suddenly a bit out of my control," says Gil. "Before I got a new position Jeane and I discussed that we would never 'pull back' on our giving, which meant that we would always move forward with our original giving commitment. But the Lord had his hand in my job-seeking process and I was offered a wonderful new job."

The de las Alases have given regularly to CRU (formerly known as Campus Crusade for Christ), a worldwide interdenominational Christian ministry committed to helping take the Gospel of Jesus Christ to all nations, and to World Vision, a Christian humanitarian organization that works with children, families, and their communities worldwide by tackling the root causes of poverty and injustice. They also support their church's global church-planting mission and are focused on new ways to invest in Christian education. "The mission of our children's school is to grow lifetime followers of Christ," says Gil. "We want to help instill this in other children at a very young age."

In addition to talking with their own children about giving, the couple wants to expose them directly to what they're doing. When the de las Alases hosted a lunch at their house for a CRU missionary, the children were interested in knowing why a stranger was coming into their house and talking to the group. "It's important that they see that giving is not always about just writing a check, but can include taking action to help others raise money for their ministries," says Gil. "We all know that children learn as much from what they see as from what we tell them."

Jeane, who describes herself as "thrifty," says that her and Gil's backgrounds keep them grounded. "We don't want to live larger than we need to. And we know that we're not supposed to lay up treasures here on earth. At the end of the day what do you want to leave as your legacy? We want our legacy to be giving to organizations that are going to bring life to other people. We have a budget for what we need to live on and the rest is going to God. It's His anyway."

# TWENTY ONE

## WE HAVEN'T BEEN
# ABLE TO
# OUT GIVE GOD

### MONYA & DAVID GILES
*Austin, Texas*

"It has been a journey we never imagined. I grew up on a farm with holes in my blue jeans. I never saw myself 'here.' We have a nice old house and a nice little yard and a woodworking shop. That's really all we need."

The journey that David Giles describes is one that has taken him and his wife, Monya, from a young married couple with the typical struggles of career, finances, and raising kids to a place where they have literally given it all away.

> "We weren't able — then or later — to out give God."

As a 30-year-old, David started as a manufacturers' representative in Houston, Texas, selling combustion equipment. With that first company, he experienced unexpected success. "As an independent sales rep, you can do pretty well," says David. "After a while, though, the business was making more money than I had ever imagined. That's when we got connected to Crown Financial Ministries and began living our lives by their principles, one of which is God owns it all, and we are only stewards of God's possessions. We began donating to multiple causes and more money seemed to just keep coming in."

Says Monya, "We weren't able — then or later — to out give God. It didn't matter how much we gave away, He just kept pouring more in to us."

After years in Houston, David and Monya moved north of Austin, where David started a company, making equipment for the oil industry. "I thought of it as a retirement hobby," says David. "But it really took off — my hobby ended up being more successful than anything else I'd done. I was praying that God would actually unload this successful hobby by sending me a partner. He did, and I turned my attention to the next thing."

David and Monya had been long-time clients of the National Christian Foundation (NCF), a non-profit group that helps generous givers simplify their giving, multiply their impact, and experience the joy of sending more to their favorite causes than they ever dreamed possible. The organization's mission is to mobilize resources by inspiring biblically-based generosity. With the daily burden of running an unexpectedly successful "hobby business" off David's shoulders, the couple changed their giving strategy. Rather than income coming to them and them giving it to NCF after they paid taxes, they contacted NCF to set up a donor advised fund. To fund the new giving strategy, David gave 40% of his company's ongoing revenue to the NCF fund; 50% of the company went to his partner.

"Not only does the income bypass us, it allowed us to name our two daughters, two sons-in-law, and our son as the board of directors for the fund," says David. "They are responsible for researching the causes we want to fund and finding causes they believe in and want to fund themselves. Our children have taken responsibility for this, and with a true passion. Not only do they provide direction for our NCF funds, but they have taken on their own personal charitable giving."

One of the causes David and Monya consider very dear to them is Relief Network Ministries, founded in 2001 in League City, Texas, with a mission to help end the water crisis in Nigeria. The organization's over-arching goal is to significantly reduce the cycle of poverty and disease attributable to the water crisis. It focuses on ways to alleviate the adverse consequences of poverty and illiteracy, such as poor hygienic standards and inadequate skills for gainful employment. Relief Network Ministries' motto is "Water 4 Life in Jesus' Name." David and Monya got an interesting first introduction to the founder of Relief Network Ministries, Ambrose Ochiabuto Sunny Okorie.

"In Houston, we went to a mid-sized church," says David. "One Sunday, a man in full Nigerian garb came in. He certainly stood out from our normal crowd. That's when I first met Sunny and began to get to know him. Sunny and Relief Network drill about 15 to 20 water wells each year in Niger and Nigeria. Because he's well known for his work with the wells, he gets a chance to preach in churches. He told stories about three or four hundred people coming to Christ after he preached. I thought surely he was exaggerating, but he's not. I got independent verification on those numbers. Sunny leverages his well drilling into preaching and soul salvation — it's a full package and it is our favorite charity as far as return on investment."

When David and Monya reflect back on their years of giving, they point to the teachings of Crown Financial Ministries. "We began living by the Crown principles that God owns it ALL! God requires a tenth, but He is more interested to see what you do with the remaining 90% He has given you to steward," says Monya. "We never saw God fail us — even when our son, Michael, was diagnosed with a brain tumor at the age of seven. We were secure in the knowledge, all through Michael's treatments, that God had a greater interest in our son than we did — we were only the stewards. Kind of like Abraham with Isaac, we had to trust that God knew best — whatever the outcome. Everything belongs to God, not just money."

The coolest thing, say David and Monya, is that the "giving legacy" has been passed on to their children. "It has been wonderful to hear their stories of supporting people and causes — they have a real heart for giving. Oh, they certainly heard us go on and on for years about building up treasures in heaven and why we do what we do with our giving. Our children understand the difference in needs and wants. Because they can say 'I don't need that' it's easy for them to give. When we first made our will years ago, our children were small and it took us a while to figure out that the worst thing we could do was to give them too much money. We have a lot of blessings from being poor in our younger years. We did not have a refrigerator or stove for our first six months of marriage. There are lots of memories and lessons we learned. We don't want to deny them the blessings and memories that their own hard work can bring. Giving them too much or leaving too much could cause harm, so we choose to give it away instead."

# TWENTY TWO

# LIFE
## IS A
# MISSION
# FIELD

---

### CORINNE & ERIC GOKCEN
*Philadelphia, Pennsylvania*

To see a young boy do normal things like walking and running is not typically a cause for sweet relief and gratitude. But for Eric and Corinne Gokcen, to see "their" Mohammed do those things is.

Mohammed represents everything that the Gokcens have dedicated most of their adult lives to, ever since Eric finished his medical residency in orthopedic surgery. At first, they only took short-term medical mission trips — to Russia, Belarus, and Botswana — but longed for another way for Eric to respond to the calling in his heart. "I wanted to practice orthopedics after seeing the extensive need for medical attention in the areas I went to, but couldn't see how that could be accomplished in remote and developing areas," says Eric.

$$\left\{ \begin{array}{c} \text{"Through healing, we get to} \\ \text{show them the God who hasn't} \\ \text{cursed them, but the God} \\ \text{who loves them dearly."} \end{array} \right\}$$

An accountant friend at the Gokcens' church was sent to do an audit of an organization called CURE International. Knowing Eric's heart for medical missions, she picked up some brochures and passed them along to him. "When I saw what CURE did, I was very interested," says Eric. CURE, based in Lemoyne, Pennsylvania, serves children who, because of their disabilities, are often the very last: The last to be included. The last to be protected from abuse. The last to be afforded dignity. And, sometimes, even the last to be given food in their own homes. CURE believes that healing changes everything, not only because it brings an end to physical pain but because it means restoration of dignity, protection from abuse, and inclusion in family, school, and culture. The children CURE serves have conditions such as clubfoot, bowed legs, cleft lips, untreated burns, and hydrocephalus. CURE is also highly focused on the spiritual health of the children it serves. "Often, these children are told that their condition is due to a curse," says Corinne. "Through healing, we get to show them the God who hasn't cursed them, but the God who loves them dearly."

At the time the Gokcens learned of CURE, the organization had several hospitals in Africa and Central America. Interestingly, Eric and Corinne had missionary friends working in a town just north of CURE's hospital in Kijabe, Kenya. They felt the Lord was telling them to go, so in 2004 they visited Kijabe, and went again in 2005. Following the 2005 trip, Eric says, "I really felt that God was asking us to join CURE full time and move to Kenya." In August of 2006, Eric left his private practice in Pennsylvania and he and Corinne and their daughter moved to Kenya, while their son stayed behind to attend college.

> "His whole life is being transformed, even though it's still unfolding."

Eric's work in Kenya allowed him to fulfill God's calling on his life by caring for disabled children, performing surgery, and leading clinics throughout Kenya. He was also instrumental in launching an orthopedic training program in that country. Corinne worked at the hospital, praying with the children and their parents and being "the great encourager." After two years in Kenya, the Gokcens were asked to move to Ethiopia to help set up a new hospital there. After much prayer, they moved to Addis Ababa, Ethiopia, in November 2008. They wrestled with the decision but became convinced that the Lord wanted them in a place with 80 million people — many in severe poverty — and a desperate need for doctors. That's when Mohammed came into their lives.

At age 10, it was all but impossible for Mohammed to move, much less walk or run. He had suffered severe burns when he fell into a fire at 8 months old, living since then with intense pain and continual bleeding. It was difficult for his family to care for him and through an amazing series of events he made his way to the capital city and the CURE hospital. "We did several surgeries on Mohammed," says Eric. "After successfully healing, he could actually stand on both feet for the first time in his life." Even better, because of the loving "Jesus kind of care" that he received, Mohammed prayed to receive Jesus. He also joined the Gokcen family for a while, living with them for almost a year. "It became clear to us that God was asking us to bring him into our home, so that's what we did. We got him tutors, as he had never been to school a day in his life," says Corinne. "His whole life is being transformed, even though it's still unfolding."

While at the CURE hospital in Ethiopia, Eric had the opportunity to perform surgery on a teenage girl with a very rare and unusual condition — she was a parasitic twin. Similar to a Siamese twin, a parasitic twin isn't actually two bodies joined together; rather, it is one with extra body parts from the other twin attached. In her case, she had two extra legs attached to her pelvis and some rudimentary arms attached to her abdomen. "She was ostracized by her community," recalls Eric. "No school, just hidden all the time. We were able to operate on her — there were probably six or eight different surgeons involved — and remove all of the extra body parts in a long and complex surgery. She recovered exceptionally well and is now back in school. It's been amazing to be part of stories like that, to see lives transformed every day. It never gets old."

Eric and Corinne want CURE patients to be cared for spiritually as well as medically. "Each CURE hospital has a spiritual team that speaks the native language," says Eric. "Every patient hears the Gospel while they're in the hospital."

The Gokcens returned to the U.S. in 2013, feeling the Lord calling them to a new mission field. They still remain involved with CURE and its work. In 2015, Eric was instrumental in getting accreditation from the national accreditation board for residency training in orthopedics so that Loma Linda University Hospital residents, where he was working at the time, can do a rotation at the CURE hospital in Malawi. Currently, Eric works at Temple Hospital in Philadelphia, Pennsylvania.

Corinne says there were plenty of times during their years in Africa that they fought the feeling of being overwhelmed. "Sometimes it was, 'Can I do this? Because God, this is hard.' It's difficult living among such poverty, away from friends and family, and with regular power and water outages. But we continually felt God working through us. We knew we were there because He sent us."

Eric acknowledges that because he practices orthopedic surgery daily, he still gets the joy of knowing God is using him to change people's lives — to fix bodies, alleviate chronic pain, help people return to productive lives. It was a harder transition for Corinne to leave Africa and come back to the U.S. "We regularly saw people literally crawling on the ground, and who had maybe never walked a day in their lives," she says. "And then we got to see so many people get up and walk after surgery, which is incredible to witness. When we came back and I was praying about missing that, I suddenly realized that God was telling me to notice the 'crawlers' right here. They just don't look the same, but they're crawling through life, either emotionally or spiritually. To look through the lens of God is to see what the mission is now. One of my sayings is 'Life is a mission field.' It's all about seeing it in front of you."

# TWENTY THREE

## WORKING TO

# END MODERN DAY SLAVERY

**SUE & JEFF PANKRATZ**
*Silver Spring, Maryland*

When most people think of the word "justice," they likely think of a courtroom. Or of Justitia, the blindfolded Roman goddess who holds scales and a sword and usually stands outside a courtroom. But justice can also come in a field of crops or at a brick kiln in remote areas of northern India. In these cases, justice meant freedom for 393 bonded labor victims — toddlers to elderly people — who were rescued by Justice Ventures International (JVI) and its partners.

$$\left\{ \begin{array}{c} \ldots \text{an organization devoted} \\ \text{to ending modern day slavery} \\ \text{and other extreme injustice.} \end{array} \right\}$$

JVI and its important work is the result of the passionate and determined hearts of Sue and Jeff Pankratz, who long ago were drawn to the suffering and needs of the poor — and the poorly served — overseas and in inner-city America. It is, pure and simple, an organization devoted to ending modern day slavery and other extreme injustice. Sue, a primary care physician, was involved in evangelism and discipleship ministries in East Asia in the mid-1980s before she met and married Jeff, a lawyer, who had been involved in justice issues in inner-city Los Angeles after college. After they married and moved to Indianapolis, they decided to move into an urban neighborhood; both got involved in ministries for the poor — Sue helping to start an inner-city medical clinic and Jeff founding a non-profit organization called Community Organization Legal Assistance Project. They moved to Washington, D.C. in 1999 where they continued to be involved in work among the urban poor. In 2003, a leave of absence from their jobs for a one-year assignment in India with International Justice Mission (IJM) completely changed their lives.

"When we came back from India, it was hard to get the experience and the needs off of our minds," says Jeff. "We saw so much of the severe injustice of human trafficking and so many of the desperately poor in the mega-cities. But we also saw a lot of great work being done by leaders in local churches, businesses, and non-profit organizations. In 2007, we founded JVI. Our idea was to partner with various local organizations to help them do the work of bringing freedom, justice, and restoration to the poor and oppressed. We're a small organization, but through partnership at the local level we have been able to make a significant impact with the resources God has given us."

That impact is seen in the life-changing rescue of more than 200 people in the Indian state of Uttar Pradesh. In May 2016, JVI partnered with local government authorities and the People's Vigilance Committee on Human Rights to secure the freedom of 207 bonded labor victims working in deplorable conditions in a brick kiln operation and suffering terrible abuse at the hands of the owners. "Requests for rest, more food or proper wages were met with vicious beatings from the owners," says Sue. "None of the 113 children on site attended school. Instead, children as young as three to four years of age were given grueling tasks to do at the kiln."

In January 2015, JVI had successfully undertaken one of its largest rescues, freeing 186 people, including 38 entire families, from the kamiya system, multi-generational bonded slavery in the agricultural sector. Those held captive and forced to work lived in small huts made of dry grass and were given tiny portions of grains every day as their only food. After helping enslaved workers get their freedom, JVI works to see that offenders are prosecuted and that those freed are paid back wages and have access to rehabilitation funds through the government.

JVI has four areas of emphasis. The first is to secure justice for victims through legal case work, primarily through local lawyers. Second is to provide human rights training, which includes local leaders of non-governmental organizations, community leaders, and government officials. "We train prosecutors and government administrations," says Jeff. "In India, we recently trained more than 240 judges. Most of the local governments are quite receptive to the work we're doing, although we've certainly met some resistance. But in many areas, we've found ways to link arms with the government, working with local leaders that really care about making changes."

JVI's third focus is rights-based advocacy, linking up with other organizations to promote broader systemic change. Finally, JVI works with what are called "freedom businesses," small businesses, usually exporters, that market and sell products made by human trafficking survivors. Freedom businesses also means sponsoring micro-business activity — JVI and partners recently provided more than 80 former bonded laborers with sewing machines, goats, bicycles, and transport cars. "These investments offer a new form of freedom: the dignified opportunity to earn an income and provide a better life for their families," says Sue.

The issue of human trafficking is often invisible to most of us, but it's a serious and devastating problem around the world. "India has close to 14 million enslaved people, the most in the world," says Jeff. "China is second, with about 3 million. As far as the urban poor, India and China are home to many of the world's mega-cities. In Mumbai, for example, about 10 million people, out of a population of 20 million, live in squatter settlements, which have dangerous, abusive, and oppressive conditions. In China, unprecedented migration from rural areas to cities has resulted in large numbers of urban poor who are subject to very abusive labor practices."

Even though JVI is not an evangelistic organization, Sue and Jeff see reaching people who are un-reached as a satisfying benefit of their work. "Our partner-ships on justice in hard-to-reach areas tend to be a real opening for sharing about the love of Jesus Christ," says Sue. One of their partners, New India Evangelistic Association (NIEA), reached out to the Muslim population in an area that had experienced devastated flooding. Tens of thousands were left homeless and in refugee camps. Sue was part of the medical team treating people in the camps. Leaders of the village allowed them to show The Jesus Film and, amazingly, the Muslim leaders invited the team from NIEA to come and start a church in their village. "It was because of the love and mercy shown in God's name," Sue says.

The Pankratzes have three daughters who lived with them in India during their time there. "They were all very involved in our work in the slum areas of India," says Sue. "Our girls have seen, in a very direct way, what poverty looks like. It certainly had an impact and is affecting their choices now as young adults."

Even when the number of people freed is small, it's a victory for JVI. Recently, JVI helped free two young women in a rural area near Bengal from forced pros-titution. Working once again with a local partner, JVI helped the organization document the case and bring it forward for prosecution. "Freedom of 'just' two people is obviously important for those two, but it has a ripple effect," says Jeff. "Our work helps sensitize local governments so that they're more likely to take appropriate action when they see other cases of human trafficking."

While the Pankratzes no doubt have plenty of Scripture verses they could point to that illustrate their work and inspire them, a favorite one is 2 Corinthians, 3:17 — "Where the spirit of the Lord is, there is freedom."

# TWENTY FOUR

# BELIEVING BIG

### TO FACE, FIGHT, AND

# OVERCOME
# CANCER

**IVELISSE & JIMMY PAGE**
*Baltimore, Maryland*

When Ivelisse was diagnosed with colon cancer at age 37, it was a shock, even though her father had passed away of the same disease at age 39. How could it be? She was "doing all the right things" — eating organic food, exercising, and having regular colonoscopies because of her high-risk status. After two surgeries, the second because the cancer spread to her liver, Ivelisse had only an 8% chance of surviving her cancer.

"When we learned the final diagnosis, emotions took over," Ivelisse said. "I was filled with fear, wondering what would happen to my kids if they had to grow up without a mom. It was especially painful because I grew up without a dad. I was confronted with the question of whether or not I would let this fear take over."

> They needed to stop living in fear and turn to the best cure that they knew: God's Word.

Ivelisse and her husband, Jimmy, knew that battling cancer would take more than just good medical care. They needed to stop living in fear and turn to the best cure that they knew: God's Word. Jimmy compiled a list of Scripture passages into a prayer for Ivelisse that they dubbed the "I Will Have No Fear Prayer."

"God's Word gives peace," Ivelisse says. "We battled our fear with the Word." Throughout her fight against cancer, Ivelisse kept the "I Will Have No Fear Prayer" close to remind herself of the truth of God's Word. Soon that simple prayer would form the cornerstone of a life-changing ministry. But first, Ivelisse needed to find the treatment plan that would work for her.

Convinced that traditional chemotherapy wouldn't help her much — given the dismal odds she faced — and, in fact, realizing that it might even make her final months more miserable, Ivelisse found a doctor who practiced "complementary medicine." He introduced her to cancer therapy using mistletoe extract, which is allowed under homeopathic guidelines if administered by a physician trained in natural medicine. What Ivelisse discovered was that mistletoe had been used around the world for more than 100 years — in malignant and non-malignant tumors, for stimulation of bone marrow activity, for reducing the risk of tumor recurrence and alongside conventional treatments to offset the side effects of chemotherapy and radiation. "A huge benefit," says Ivelisse, "is that because it can minimize side effects of conventional treatment, people can have a much better quality of life as they are going through a very difficult treatment."

> "God has us here for a reason. Let's try and be a light and bring encouragement to this dark place."

People going through difficult treatments actually sparked the first idea that the Pages had for helping others. "When Jimmy and I were sitting in the waiting room, we looked around and all we saw were faces filled with fear and anxiety — What was the doctor going to share? What are those tests going to show? We looked at each other one day and said, 'You know what? God has us here for a reason. Let's try and be a light and bring encouragement to this dark place.'" Ivelisse's idea for being a light in a dark place took shape when she was drinking one morning from a hand-painted mug one of her children made. "I used it every morning because it made me smile," she recalls. "I said to myself, 'Mugs — that's what we'll do.' I also had so many friends asking what they could do to help, and this would be a tangible way to help. So we got a group of people together and painted and fired mugs, each with the single word 'believe' on it. Jimmy and I began handing them out to patients, hoping that the mug would offer some encouragement to them knowing that someone they didn't even know cared for them."

Ivelisse beat the 8% survival rate of stage IV colon cancer. Her oncologist at Johns Hopkins had surprisingly agreed to continue to monitor her despite her refusing chemotherapy, in large part because he saw how well they had researched her case and had fully taken all factors into consideration. One day while with him, Ivelisse expressed her belief that mistletoe therapy had helped save her life and also her frustration at why it wasn't widely available to others. She wanted a clinical trial for it — without that, it could never be considered a standard of care for cancer patients. Her doctor said, not surprisingly, "It just isn't that easy." It would take a lot of money, years of discussion, and design of protocol for a clinical trial to begin. Ivelisse and Jimmy committed to help raise the funds needed. And thus was born Believe Big, a ministry to provide resources, direction, and hope to families struggling with cancer and, perhaps most importantly, to raise the $500,000 needed for the clinical trial.

In December 2015, the intravenous mistletoe clinical trial was approved by the Food and Drug Administration (FDA) after a long review process by both the FDA and the Johns Hopkins Internal Review Board. "At Believe Big, we're so excited to be in the trenches with cancer research," says Ivelisse. "This trial is a huge step forward, as it brings the conventional and complementary medical communities together."

With a motto of "Face it, Fight it, Overcome it," Believe Big is much more than a fundraising arm for the clinical trial. Its mission is to help families navigate the cancer journey and bridge the gap between conventional and complementary medicine for fighting cancer. Believe Big educates patients on a comprehensive approach to cancer prevention and treatment, connects patients with physicians trained in mistletoe therapy, and provides spiritual support to help patients and their families overcome fear and anxiety. Believe Big also gives out wellness grants so that patients can have access to affordable complementary and alternative therapies, which are not covered by health insurance, and connects patients to clinical nutrition therapists who specialize in oncology.

Ivelisse has a team of five full-time and part-time staff, plus dozens of volunteers. They dream of a Believe Big center, where patients can find everything they need in one place — treatment, support groups, prayer, resources, and those "believe" mugs, which are still being painted and given out. But Ivelisse's biggest dream is that mistletoe therapy will one day become a standard of care for healing in the world of cancer treatment.

"I don't tell this to a lot of people, because sometimes it can sound a little crazy," Ivelisse says. "At age 13, shortly after my father died from colon cancer, I attended a summer camp. One of the camp pastors came up and told me he'd been praying and that I was going to be involved in helping find a cure for cancer. I thought that he must have heard from someone that my father died and was trying to make me feel better, but he hadn't. As the years passed I thought that the pastor must have been mistaken. But here we are, 32 years later working on a clinical trial for a treatment that could impact the way we treat cancer in America."

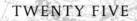

# TWENTY FIVE

# FAITHFULLY SERVING

THROUGH

# MEDICINE

AND

# EDUCATION

**SALLY & JIM SPENCER**

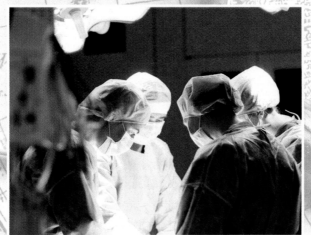

> "This, then, is how you ought to regard us: as servants of Christ and as those entrusted with the mysteries God has revealed. Now it is required that those who have been given a trust must prove faithful."
>
> 1 Corinthians 4:1 - 2, NIV

Both Jim and Sally Spencer* felt the call to mission work early in life. By high school, they both saw themselves as missionaries one day and they certainly have acted on that call, serving and working in Bangladesh, Korea, Togo, the Ukraine, and Egypt.

Their travels around the globe began after Jim went to medical school. Seeking a way to minimize medical school debt and allow Sally to stay home and raise their two children, Jim accepted a health professions scholarship from the U.S. Army, which paid his educational expenses and provided a monthly stipend. He was granted a deferment from the scholarship's required two years of service to do a five-year surgical residency, and then they were off to Korea. "We had gotten to know two couples from Korea very well while I was in my residency," says Jim. "In fact, we were able to disciple them as they came to know Christ. So we were very excited to go to Korea."

The Spencers actually think of their Army posting in Korea as their first mission-ary journey, relating it to the account of Paul in Acts 28:30-31, "For two whole years Paul stayed there in his own rented house and welcomed all who came to see him. He proclaimed the kingdom of God and taught about the Lord Jesus Christ — with all boldness and without hindrance!"

For two years, the Spencers, in partnership with a Korean friend, held a week-ly Korean/English Bible study in their living room, while also planning for their missionary lives after the Army.

The seeds of their next mission work, in Bangladesh, had been planted while Jim was in medical school. Through several contacts, they got to know other doctors who had been in Bangladesh and took two separate three-month trips there — the first while Jim was still in medical school and the second, with three children in tow, during his surgical residency. Because they developed a love for Bangladesh during those trips, Jim and Sally went to a mission candidate class and

*Pseudonyms to reflect this family's wish for remaining anonymous.*

were accepted as missionaries for an assignment after Jim's Army service ended. But Jim's father, a former pastor and professor at a Christian college, was in declining health so they delayed their departure for several months. "My dad had always said to me, 'Go to your field,'" says Jim. "He was a great encouragement to me. The day he died in October 1983 we were commissioned as missionaries from our home church. I spoke that day about my father's home-going and our going out from home."

Jim served as a staff surgeon at a hospital in Malumghat, Bangladesh, which is the major surgical resource for more than 10 million people in the region. Sally, who had always been interested in Christian education and had majored in education, began working part-time at the school for missionary children and also with the missionary education committee. She devoted much time to improving Bible correspondence courses being used in Bangladesh by organizing the first-ever conference to evaluate materials being used and create a plan to acquire or develop new courses. "Good materials are very important in a majority Muslim country such as Bangladesh," says Sally. "People need to be able to study God's Word for quite a period of time before they're at the point where they can put their faith in Christ."

If there's one thing that illustrates how Jim views medical mission work, it's something that happened regularly while the Spencers were in Bangladesh for six years. When Jim needed a respite from the demands of being almost constantly on duty, he and Sally went to a Bangladeshi friend's house in a different village. "I would ride on the back of his motorcycle to homes all around the village," says Jim. "I was caring for the sick, and he was sharing the Gospel with the family. He was the pastor driving the motorcycle and in control of where we were going, and I was God's servant riding on the back."

After returning to the U.S., Jim joined a surgical practice in New York, a group of Christian doctors who had a strong commitment to participating in medical missions. During his nine years there, Jim made several mission trips with Samaritan's Purse World Medical Mission to various third-world countries and several other trips through different organizations.

Next the Spencers found themselves called to the Ukraine. What started as a short visit turned into four more trips. In partnership with friends who had been in Ukraine for years, Jim and Sally spent time visiting with elderly Jewish holocaust survivors, and Sally had the opportunity to teach Bible classes to young trainees. But after their friends' visas were revoked when Ukraine's government went through an upheaval, "The Lord put on their hearts that they should go work in the Muslim world," says Sally. "Our friends arrived in Egypt just before the Arab Spring of 2011. In 2014, they asked me to come and teach an Old Testament overview to young Egyptian Christians. I prayed about it for many months. In particular, I was apprehensive about being accepted as a woman teacher in a male-dominated culture and I was concerned about the need to provide care for my mother who had come to live with us. God provided for every detail! We went, and it was a wonderful time! Christians in Egypt have been oppressed and marginalized, but the Holy Spirit is at work in their lives and they're very hungry to know God and have hope for the future."

In 2006, the Spencers settled in Indiana. Sally works with a ministry that shares the Gospel with international students and visiting scholars who are professors in their own countries studying in the U.S. Jim continues his work as a physician, now working in an urgent care center after 14 years of practicing emergency medicine. Opportunities to serve the Lord are still part of the Spencers' life. Jim has recently completed his 12th trip to work in mission hospitals in Togo, West Africa. This trip was his 18th with World Medical Mission. Neuropathy in his legs now keeps him from standing for long periods as is often required for surgery, so Jim uses his skills in clinic work and hospital ward rounds.

When the couple reflects on their many years as medical and educational missionaries around the world, Jim thinks back to early decisions they made. "God wants each of us to use all of our talents to help build His kingdom. We started way back when we made decisions that would help us avoid large medical school debt, so that we'd be free to serve the Lord. We knew that debt would tie us down, and I would have to settle into a practice to pay it back. Then we'd feel stuck and probably not go where we felt called. There were many ways over the years in which God used our family, our relationships with people, our money, and our time to further His kingdom. We're past 'traditional' retirement age now, but we hope that we can continue to be active in faithfully serving the Lord."

# TWENTY SIX

FINDING THE TRUE

# JOY OF GIVING

THROUGH

# PERSONAL CONNECTIONS

**ANICA & ANDY ISCH**
*Indianapolis, Indiana*

S urgeons, particularly those who are trauma surgeons, face extraordinary challenges all the time, but they don't often come with a sign from God.

Early in his career, surgeon Andy Isch encountered a personal challenge — outside the operating room — when he was urged by his financial advisor to recognize and truly own the fact that all of our resources belong to God. Coming out of medical school and residency debt-free, Andy was in a position to begin saving, investing, and giving. An opportunity presented itself and, says Andy, "I felt like God wanted me to give what at the time seemed like a really large amount. I struggled with it — Is it wise? Or is it crazy? I wanted to, and yet I didn't want to. But it also seemed very clear to me that giving this specific amount was what I should do."

> "I felt an overwhelming joy that God would give me the opportunity to do something like that."

A week later, Andy received an unexpected bonus from his surgical practice. It was the exact dollar amount as the amount he had just given. "It felt like God saying to me, 'See — you just can't out give me.' It was an amazing experience that totally changed my perspective because I gave as God led me to give. I felt a real sense of freedom."

Another "aha" moment for Andy was during a trip to China in 2005 with Walk Thru the Bible. Andy had donated to help the organization develop a new curriculum on love, sex, and relationships. Young Christian leaders had driven up to 18 hours from rural areas all over China to meet with Andy's group and were ecstatic to receive the materials. "We didn't know if the curriculum would be what they needed, but they were thrilled," says Andy. "For me, this was the reality of all of my hard work through medical school and residency training right in front of me. All those years had given me the ability to give money for something, and now it was concrete. Here we are in the middle of a communist country talking about dating and sex and marriage in a Christian context. I felt an overwhelming joy that God would give me the opportunity to do something like that. It was certainly an embodiment of the saying that it's more blessed to give than to receive."

Now an experienced giver, Andy and his wife, Anica, share the philosophy that they enjoy giving more when they have a personal relationship with the organization or ministry that is the recipient of their gift. The Isches are strategic givers, feeling that they can be more effective by giving to only a few organizations and "going deeper" rather than giving to a dozen or more. One of those organizations for which they have a personal passion is Bridge to Europe, run by Andy's friend, Beni Lup. Bridge to Europe works to combat human trafficking — modern day slavery — in Romania, an abominable practice in which people profit from the control and the exploitation of others. Unbelievably, there are more people in slavery today than in any other time in history. The U.S. Department of Health and Human Services says that human trafficking is the fastest growing criminal industry in the world. Thousands from Romania are being exploited every year because Romania is a gateway from Eastern Europe into the European Union for the export of young girls and boys. Often, the ones being rescued from the grips of traffickers have no safe place to be rehabilitated, something that Bridge to Europe plans to change, even in its own small way.

> ... feeling that they can be more effective by giving to only a few organizations and "going deeper" rather than giving to a dozen or more.

"Bridge to Europe is building the Butterfly Center, a safe house and rehabilitation facility that will address the spiritual, physical, mental, and social needs of those rescued," says Anica. "It's wonderful to be part of this organization — we're both on the Board — and to visit and see the work Bridge to Europe is doing." The Butterfly Center will have residential areas, a clinic, counseling areas, and an arts and crafts studio.

The Isches are also faithful supporters of Walk Through the Bible, a ministry that seeks to ignite a passion for God's Word through innovative live events and small group curricula. They also are heavily involved with Ravi Zacharias International Ministries (RZIM), a ministry that prioritizes reaching college and university students, potential leaders of the next generation, to explain the Gospel to skeptical audiences and equip believers on campus to share and defend their faith in the academic arena. Anica was drawn to the mission of Dr. Zacharias's ministry after hearing him speak at Taylor University in Indiana, where she went to school. Andy had also become familiar with RZIM before he met Anica. In the summer of 2015, the Isches went to an RZIM study week at The Queen's College at Oxford University in England for an intense week of training in evangelism and apologetics. "We both feel very drawn to the ministry of RZIM," says Andy.

The three primary organizations they support, in addition to their own church, give them the opportunity to truly practice being relationally involved with causes. "We want to have long-term partnerships with organizations," says Anica. "Even though we both were familiar with these ministries before we were married, they are now our causes as a couple. We feel it's very important to understand the stresses that money issues can put on a couple. As newlyweds, I believe we both feel very good about where we are as a couple committed to giving."

# TWENTY SEVEN

GIVING
# HOPE:
FROM
# ONE FARMER TO
# ANOTHER

**BECKI & TOM THOMPSON**
*Forest City, Iowa*

Often, farming is a family affair. For Becki and Tom Thompson of Forest City, Iowa, farming and giving are both family affairs. The Thompsons, long-time corn and soybean farmers in northern Iowa, say they're basically retired, yet they still help their farm manager oversee a 2,600 acre farming operation. They also have a seed plant that conditions soybean seeds for other farmers. As "serial farmers," the Thompsons sold their initial farming business and set up a foundation through the National Christian Foundation (NCF) so they could, as they put it, "give meaningful gifts to respond to what's on people's hearts." When they sold their second farming business, they set up another foundation — a family foundation so their three sons and 11 grandchildren could be involved. "God has been very good to us," says Tom. "He has blessed us beyond what we deserve and we want to give generously back to Him."

$$\left[ \text{"He has blessed us beyond what we deserve and we want to give generously back to Him."} \right\}$$

The Thompsons meet as a family with their sons and their daughters-in-law at least once a year to talk about and make plans for their giving. Two sons have formal roles in the family foundation — as treasurer and legal counsel — but the purpose of the family meetings is "to see where everybody's heart is," says Becki. "We do give locally in addition to internationally, including to the local Christian school where our boys went and an organization here that focuses on disabled people. The foundation helps keep our children in the giving mode. Several times, the children have wanted to give to an organization they feel strongly about, and along with their personal gift, our foundation will match it. The foundation is certainly not a replacement for what they want to give, but we do want it to help augment their gifts in certain instances."

Adds Tom, "Our sons have known from the time we sold our first company that we were committed to giving, and they have been fully 'on board.' In fact, they're all excited when we get together to give it away."

The Thompsons stayed close to home for one of their substantial gifts — helping fund a new athletic complex for University of Northwestern, in St. Paul, Minnesota, where all three of their sons attended. They have also given generously to

Hope 4 Kids International, a faith-based non-profit run by a close friend of theirs in Phoenix, Arizona. Hope 4 Kids serves children living in impoverished environments by establishing economic, spiritual, water, orphan, and feeding programs. It appealed to the Thompsons not only because it helps children in desperate need, but also because it's centered on the bounty that can come from land in the right hands and with the right tools. Hope 4 Kids helps villagers become productive farmers so they can grow crops, drills wells in areas where there's no clean drinking water, builds small churches, parsonages for the pastors, and medical clinics.

> "This organization really exemplifies the spirit of Jesus, showing that all children are worthy of a prosperous life and a bright future."

The Thompsons feel strongly about Hope 4 Kids' vision: Healing and empowering destitute communities with hope and necessary care to raise a new generation of healthy individuals who can break the generational curse of extreme poverty. "They build on the four pillars of hope — health, dignity, joy, and love," says Tom. "This organization really exemplifies the spirit of Jesus, showing that all children are worthy of a prosperous life and a bright future."

Hope 4 Kids also helps Ugandan women learn to become more self-sufficient through its "Victory Gardens" program, providing funds and seeds to a Ugandan ministry partner. The use of oxen and plows helps the women with their gardens, which now number 1,500 throughout Uganda. The organizational umbrella also includes Water 4 Kids, Education 4 Kids, Hope 4 Women, and Dress a Girl Around the World.

The Thompsons' sons also believe in the mission of Hope 4 Kids — in fact, two sons have been on trips to Ugandan villages supported by the organization, helping with farm tool donations so the villagers could learn to grown their own crops. Tom and Becki also hope to one day travel to see firsthand some of the farmland their giving has made possible.

# PHOTO NOTES

We are grateful for all of the photos the participants and organizations involved in this project provided to us. We truly feel these images make the stories come to life. There are a few photos that provide specific images of people or places referenced in the stories that we thought the readers might enjoy knowing about.

### GETTLE
Page 1 - Photo of Dr. Gettle examining a patient in the field hospital during the response to Typhoon Haiyan in the Philippines.

Page 4 - A picture of the field hospital up and running in Ecuador following the earthquake in April 2016.

### GARCIA
Page 25 – St. Louis Cardinals photo courtesy of https://commons.wikimedia.org/wiki/File:DSC03300_Jaime_Garc%C3%ADa.jpg per Creative Commons Attribution-Share Alike 2.0 Generic license

### BLACKWELL
Page 49 –Background image is the Edumund Pettus Bridge in Selma, AL., where the 1965 Selma to Montgomery march lead by Martin Luther King, Jr. took place.

### BROWN
Page 53 – Photo courtesy of Operation Christmas Child

### RICE
Page 65 – These photos show the baby with the bilateral white cataracts at the time of her operation and then when she came back years later for larger glasses.

Page 68 – A photo of Dr. Rice with the young man who had retinal detachment surgery and saw the working on God through the team.

### GOKCEN
Page 85 – Background image is of Mohammed taking his first steps after several surgeries.

# ACKNOWLEDGMENTS

The Faces of Generosity book began as an idea by Sandy Morgan, Director of Branding & Communications, in the summer of 2015. She shared her passion for this book with Ronald Blue & Co.'s leadership and ignited a desire to share one of the firm's key differentiators . . . we want to see our clients live a life of generosity!

Specials thanks to Malissa Light, Communications Specialist, who tirelessly worked on this project for over a year and conducted the client interviews. Without her help, this book would have never come to fruition. We owe a debt of gratitude to two outside consultants: Shelley Lee of Ashworth-Lee Communications wrote the stories, and Robert Niles of Robert Niles Design designed the cover and inside layouts for the book. But, most importantly, we want to thank our advisors for nominating the clients and the clients for spending time with us to share their unique and wonderful stories.

We hope that this book inspires each of its readers to look for the opportunities around them to give sacrificially, impact the lives of others, and seek wisdom for their wealth and their lives.